LOVE IS ALIVE

LOVE IS ALIVE

Luther Joe Thompson

Broadman Press
Nashville, Tennessee

Dewey Decimal Classification: 227.2
Subject heading: BIBLE. N. T. 1 CORINTHIANS 13
Library of Congress Catalog Number: 79-54091
Printed in the United States of America

DEDICATION

Love is such a fragile thing
As fragile as a butterfly's wing
It makes you laugh, it makes you
   sing
Or it makes you feel like a crowned
   king
It doesn't make a single sound
But you sure know when it's
   around.
                    —A Fourth-grade Child

Foreword

Why another book on love?

For centuries humankind has addressed itself to the subject. For some it has become a philosophical concept, for others an ethical principle; for some an article of faith, for others a rationale for widely differing life-styles.

In our age it has been almost an obsession—a watchword for the young, an excuse for the permissive, a gift and a demand for the religious. No word has been so bantered about, none so loosely used. Almost everyone favors it, and almost no one comprehends it. Yet no concept is so elevated, no idea so ennobling, no ethic so demanding, no reality so pervasive. Love in its highest sense reflects the very nature of God and characterizes the most satisfying life-style known to man.

The subject is one we cannot fathom, yet cannot resist. Love eludes, haunts, perplexes, yet possesses us. It dominates the New Testament and appears repeatedly in the Old Testament. It is the central focus of the biblical revelation.

More than any other word it sums up and depicts

the Christian religion. Only twice the phrase, "God is," appears in the Bible. Once we are told, "God is a Spirit" (John 4:24), and again, "God is love" (1 John 4:8). It was God's love incarnate in Jesus that astonished and dominated the first Christian believers.

The moment we make love a determinant, God becomes personal, warm, compassionate. Love is both the explanation of God's action in the world and his means for redeeming a fallen race. It is the key to understanding the pivotal doctrines of the faith, the proof of discipleship, and the only weapon of the believer. Yet it is always beyond us. It eludes us and it possesses us. We cannot live without it. In the atmosphere of love the human personality unfolds and matures. The loved child is healthier, happier, more content, more able to love other people. And it is only in the context of love that life can be reclaimed.

The most touching and profound expression of the meaning of Christian love is found in 1 Corinthians 13. Thirteen brief verses, yet comprehensive, eloquent, awe-inspiring, and revolutionary. To live in 1 Corinthians 13 is to discover a new way of life. It has been called "the portrait for which Jesus sat." To live by it is to find peace, joy, and productivity.

The first three verses present love as the one indispensable ingredient in the Christian life. The next four verses characterize love, telling what love does. The final six verses speak of love's uniqueness and permanence. I will examine it from three points of view. First, from the vantage point of what we cannot live without. Next, from what we all take for granted. And finally, from the viewpoint of eternity, that which lasts forever.

To confront life's deepest realities is to be baffled and intrigued. We cannot evade them, and yet we cannot encompass them. Their excellence defies analysis, yet we cannot live without them. Precisely because of this I waited a long time before writing this. Whatever insights I have, I offer them with the hope that some may discover anew the wonder and meaning of God's love as it works in the lives of human beings.

For two exceptional gifts I am thankful: an extraordinary congregation with whom the pilgrimage of making love tangible has been shared, and the best of all secretaries. Without them this book would not have been possible.

Our church, as a community of faith in shared pilgrimage, rediscovered the dynamic of love as we tried to live by 1 Corinthians 13. For three months, our logo, "Making Love Tangible," helped us focus on the varied facets of love in daily relationships. Week by week during that time, we directed our energies toward sharing love: parents to children and children to parents; making love tangible to in-laws, employees, those who serve us, children, teenagers, senior adults, those who love the church, and those who reject it. Together we learned that love lives and gives life.

—LUTHER JOE THOMPSON

Contents

1. What the World Needs Now

"Tell me whom you love and I will tell you what you are."

—Arsene Houssaye

He was young, idealistic, determined to make his contribution, but he found the processes of democracy painfully slow and complicated. For every solution he suggested, there were at least two varying opinions. Even when there was agreement, there was an obstinate reluctance to act. Finally, in desperation, the young man exclaimed, "How do you expect us to find a solution? We don't even agree on the problem!" And then, somewhat wistfully, he added, "That there is something wrong, I know. But what do you do about it?"

The frustration and hope is reflected in the lyrics of a popular song—to the effect that "what the world needs now is love." Is it mere nostalgia and sentiment, or is it true? What does the world need now?

There are many differing opinions. Ask any dozen people you meet. A young woman says, "More eligible men," and an unattached man reacts with, "More marriageable women." Responses include: "More social security," "A good five-cent cigar," "Less women's lib," "Moral leadership," "Someone to inspire and challenge us," "The old-time religion," "More gasoline," "People

who want to work," "A renewed emphasis on integrity
and honesty," "Peace on earth," "Safety on our
streets," "More fun." The list is endless. If the items
made in jest and those which reflect a basic self-cen-
teredness are eliminated, all the others are essentially
a reflection of what the New Testament calls *agape*.
Maybe this is not what the songwriter had in mind.
Did he mean sex, romance, or devotion—something
received or something given?

The fundamental problem with our English word
"love" is its ambiguity. Perhaps nothing is so taken
for granted and so little understood in the context of
Christian faith as the word "love."

We say, "God is love," never stopping to examine
the implications of what we have said. We sing, "I love
to tell the story," knowing full well that we may never
mention faith to our neighbor who lives across the
street. We speak of loving other people, and proceed
to manipulate, maneuver, and use them for our own
selfish ends.

Sensual love may be nothing more than glandular
indulgence and bodily satisfaction. The man who loves
a woman so intensely in the moment of passion may
spurn her once his sexual desire has been satisfied. "I
love you," may mean, in all sorts of subtle ways, "I
love me and want you." Nearly always, sexual promis-
cuity is an evidence of a kind of love addiction, a compulsion to prove charm, attraction, or potency—men
and women trying to reassure themselves they are
loved.

"Parental love," so-called, may not be love at all.
Consider the mother who talks so much about how
she loves her emotionally damaged son, but refuses

to let him see a physician. And why? For fear the doctor might expose her unresolved guilt and immaturity which had caused the problem in the first place. Parents who say to the psychiatrist, "Cure my kid, but don't touch me," don't love their child—they love themselves! Then there is the effusive, vague, self-righteous "I-love-everybody; let's-pray-for-the-world" variety. It's a pious fraud, as cheap as it's phony, and it drives many a candid and honest person away from the church.

Perhaps the place to start is with what love is not. The Greek word used almost exclusively in the New Testament for God's kind of love is *agape*. Now why did Paul and John and the others choose that rather than *eros* or *storge* or *philia*?

Among the Greeks *agape* was the least-used of the four, yet it is the most widely used in the New Testament. Clearly, it was chosen to express the New Testament writers' understanding of Christian love. It had to do with the will and conveys an interest in helping others. Love in the New Testament is radically redefined in terms of Jesus himself. It reflects the cross. "*Agape* is used to express the spontaneous, creative, caring love that is expressive of God's nature and that extended to undeserving men in Christ." [1] It is the love learned from Jesus.

To say "God is love" is to say more than "God loves." Nor can the statement be reversed to read "Love is God." God is always the measure of love, never love the measure of God. *Agape* represents love that has its source in God and it is love by choice. "Love is centered in concern for others . . . To follow the way of love is to follow the very nature of God." [2]

Now in this light Christian love is not what many assume it to be. There may be elements of Christian love in these things, but in their essence they are not the same as Christian love. Christian love is not sexual passion. Sexuality is one of God's good gifts, and life is impoverished to believe otherwise. But *agape* is more than sexuality; indeed *agape* undergirds and controls sexual passion if it is Christian.

Christian love is not sentimentality or pleasant feelings. These are good and we need them, but *agape* is more. Christian love is neither family loyalty nor mere compatibility; neither common interest nor preference in the exercise of taste. It is neither a pact between friends, as meaningful as that is, nor mere charity. Charity can be condescending, and even cruel, if exercised to meet the needs of the giver. *Agape* is not religious devotion, as fine as that may be, and certainly it is not a beautiful abstraction.

When the word *agape* is used in this book, it calls attention to the qualities singular to Christian love. This radical kind of love is one of the most powerful forces on earth.

To talk about love is sometimes to shadow it, make it suspect. Love acts. It does something! It listens. It hears. It identifies with. It tries to understand. It desires to help. It gives and shares and cares. It makes itself vulnerable. It is a spendthrift! Do you recall the old proverb: "If you have to tell your children you love them, you don't!"? There is certainly something synthetic and false about the man who is always talking about how much he loves Christ. It's like boasting about humility or parading generosity or advertising thanksgiving. Love doesn't talk—it acts. Love is something you do!

What do we mean by *agape?* This is the term the apostle Paul uses in 1 Corinthians 13 and the apostle John uses in the fourth and fifth chapters of his first epistle. Both of them saw love as the primary and indispensable element in the Christian experience. From Jesus both of them had learned what they knew and told about love; in him they had seen love in the flesh. *Agape* is the "God kind of love," love that finds its source and motivation, its measure and meaning in God himself.

The Greeks considered it self-evident that the gods did not love. Why should they since they lack nothing? And further, to be concerned or compassionate about man would make the gods vulnerable, less than perfect.

Yet the Greeks were among the most precise in defining what love means. In the New Testament alone there are four different words used for love. There is *storge* which refers essentially to family love, love of parent for child and child for parent. "A child," Plato says, "loves and is loved by those who brought him into the world."

Eros is basically the love of a man for a woman, and there is always passion involved. In all fairness it should be made clear that Plato also had a much nobler conception of *eros*. For him it was more than earthly, sensual love. It was desire, aspiration, longing, love for the beautiful and the good. When a man glimpses the beautiful and the good, the idea in the things, he is seized by *eros*, the longing for possession. It is that which drives the soul in the direction of the ideal world.

But even at best it is self-centered.

"Philia" is the warmest and best Greek word for love. Warm, tender affection. The love of deep and abiding friendship.

"Agape" is unconquerable benevolence, invincible goodwill. This is God's character. He makes his sun to shine upon the evil and the good. *Agape* is the power to love those whom we do not like or who do not like us. Not merely something of the heart, rather of will, a determination of the mind—an unconquerable goodwill even to those who hurt and injure us. Such love makes a man like God. In God there is universal goodness, even toward persons who have broken his law and broken his heart. *Agape* is love so noble, so divine that Christianity alone gave it meaning.

Before Jesus came men did not generally recognize God as a God of love. To the ancient Jew he was a God of power, majesty, holiness, and even goodness, but never the involved and vulnerable one. To imagine the gods loving men was simply illogical to the Greeks. To the Romans, deity cared only to avenge. We sometimes forget how startlingly original John 3:16 really is. To say "God is love" is to declare that love is God's characteristic activity. If he creates, he creates in love; if he rules, he rules in love; if he judges, he judges in love. All that he does is an expression of his nature which is love. The consequences of this truth are endless.

God is love! It is amazing how many doors that single statement unlocks. It tells us something fundamental about the universe, providence, pain and suffering, the meaning and purpose of our existence, redemption, and everlasting life. It is a key to the whole of the

Christian life. It is the controlling attribute of God himself. It is the condition and the sign of sonship—the only valid proof of discipleship. It is the key to understanding the great doctrines of the Holy Scriptures: providence, judgment, eternal punishment, grace, eternal life. It is the weapon of the believer. It is God's means for redeeming the human race. It is the most powerful force in the world. Augustine called Christianity the religion of love. For him love was the criterion for all things Christian. "Love God," he said, "and do as you please." Calvin held that every promise of God is an attestation of His love!

Agape is to love as God loves. What the world needs now is not more sex, more indulgence, more pleasure, more comfort, more leisure, more wealth, but more character, more integrity, more understanding, more brotherly kindness, more faith in God. And if I read my Bible correctly, this is what *agape* is all about.

To make love an end in itself is to destroy it. When you say "God is love," you say the costliest thing that could be said about God. Why would God endure us with our failures and foibles, our coldness and our rebellion, our bigotry and our hostility? Not because of our worth, but because of his love. He does for us what we cannot do for ourselves, simply because he is God.

Agape by its very nature finds tangibility inevitable. Indeed, love in the abstract is not love at all. To make it merely a theological concept, an emotional experience, or a physical sensation is to impoverish and ultimately destroy it. Love, you see, must be all-encompassing and tangible.

If I love my child, my wife, my friend, my neighbor, my dog, I must show it. I have thought so many times about my childhood Christmases during the Great Depression. I've often wondered how my parents did what they did for us. Now I know why my mother's hands so often were red and raw, and why my dad arose so early and worked so late. Their generosity to me at Christmas was sometimes purchased with their blood. Love is like that. It has no meaning unless and until it becomes tangible; and interestingly, it is its own reward, for it begets itself. There is an old Irish proverb: "Money will buy a fine dog, but only love will make him wag his tail."

Now let us define love in terms of tangibility. First, in the language of children:

> Love is a warm feeling when you're cold.
> Love is knowing your daddy is there.
> Love is someone stooping down to where you are.
> Love is Christmas morning.
> Love is your mother when you're hurt.
> Love is having a friend.
> Love is somebody to talk to.
> Love is washing dishes.
> Love is being kind.

And then in the language of adults:

> Love is searching for something you admire in someone you dislike and letting him know it.
> Love is bread when you're hungry.
> Love is spending time with someone you know is lonely.
> Love is finding someone who wants to talk and listening to him.

Love is patience.

Love is opening the door of your heart.

Love is watching for things you can compliment in others.

Love is helping others believe in themselves.

Love is sharing what is precious to you.

Love is helping others grow.

2. The Indispensable Ingredient

"A man is not where he lives, but where he loves."

—A Latin Proverb

"We Christians must be refuse gatherers, cleaning up the dirt left by others. Followers of Christ are those who must gather up the 'unclean.' This is called redemption—cleaning up the nasty places—the cross!" [1]

These words of Toyohiko Kagawa, the astonishing Japanese Christian leader who died in 1960, exemplify his manner of living as a believer.

Kagawa tells how he learned of such love of God. A missionary knocked at his door during student days. Kagawa had left a hospital with tuberculosis and had gone to die in a hut in a fishing village. When the missionary asked permission to enter, Kagawa warned of the contagious nature of his disease. "I have something more contagious than disease," the missionary said, "I have come with the love of God." [2] The Christian came to his bedside and immediately began to minister to his need.

A loving God can only be served in a loving manner. History is filled with the stories of those believers who tried to serve God with unloving actions. We learn slowly that we cannot serve a God of love without having loving manners. *Agape,* the Christian's prime

23

weapon in waging God's warfare in the world, can have no part in clever manipulation, subtle pressure, gimmickry, duress, or torture in any form.

Hawaii, James Michener's moving historical novel, and the subsequent movie based on the book, depicts a fascinating land and poignant struggle. This fiftieth state, 2,100 miles west of California, consisting of twenty tropical islands, breathtaking in beauty and striking contrasts, weaves a story both complex and heart-rending.

As the book unfolds, it presents the arrival of missionaries from America in 1820. The dogmatism and sternness of the missionaries is dramatized and overdrawn. They could not have been all bad—for in one generation, these missionaries Christianized and made literate these gentle people, a task rarely matched in mission annals.

Yet Michener presents Reverend Hale as a stern, hard, New England puritan, his wife as gentle and loving. Overdrawn or not, they are not without parallels in Christian history. Even today, the descendants of those first missionaries' families are known as the "big five" because the missionaries grasped much of the wealth and land of these beautiful isles. We are reminded of the African who said, "The missionaries came and taught us about Jesus. They taught us to close our eyes when we prayed to God, and when we opened our eyes, they had taken all our land."

Hawaiian mission history is a poignant irony of the contrast between a Hebrew God of wrath and the friendly, loving, pagan god of the Polynesians. To what degree was the clergyman's god real and to what degree a caricature? Anyone, anytime who fails to embody God's love as He is, fails to present God. If we are dogmatic, overbearing, manipulative, greedy, we are ungodly, despite all our convictions to the contrary.

In Paul's day, so early in the life of Christianity, there were those who were divisive in the Corinthian congregation; a divisiveness reflected even in the exercise of the gifts God had given to each Christian. Gifts were being perverted into bickering and pride, self-serving and showing off.

The Christian knows that his talents are given for use, that he is paid in *kind* as he uses them for others. If you have a gift for kindness, and you use it for the Lord, he gives you more kindness—not as the recipient, but as the giver to bestow on others. If your gift is friendship, and you use this gift to make friends for the Kingdom, the talent grows.

If your talent is the ability to give money, and you give money for the use of others and the glory of God, does he then give you more money? No! Your talent is the *giving*, not the money, and you are paid in *kind*. You will become increasingly generous, finding more and more ways to give of yourself and your money. Thus your talent will be multiplied, and I might add— so is your joy!

Paul writes to the Corinthians that there is a more excellent way to use their gifts, and it is the best way of all. He does not say that love is "the greatest thing in the world." Rather, he says it is the greatest gift given to the Christian. Love is the greatest gift and the one that controls all others. To follow the way of love is to follow the nature of God himself. Love is the best way of all because it is God's way; without it nothing we do has power.

Whatever your gift—teaching or preaching, singing or playing, organizing or expediting, business or planning, working with your hands or with your mind, keeping buildings or serving meals—as you work or perform, you need to do so in love, or it is meaningless in God's sight.

"Love makes all things new," the Franciscans tell us, and love does make things new. This love is costly, demanding, and not always the easiest way of all. By its very nature, *agape* focuses on the other person. Much of our conversation concerning love involves our search for something or someone. It is only natural to wish to be loved, cared for, understood. But to love in the Christian manner is to arrive at the place in life when we accept the fact that God loves us, and we are done with self-concern. Then we can minister to others in love. We need to resist our own obsession with being loved as we would the devil himself.

The portrait Jesus sat for in 1 Corinthians 13 gives characteristics that we can contemplate for a lifetime. It is so vast and inexhaustible, a symphony of praise, an oratorio of beauty and truth. As Paul comes to the end of his declaration, he becomes lyrical. There is form, symmetry, sequence, and progression. Here is exultation in a pattern for a lifetime. A mere thirteen verses, this passage speaks of the supremacy of love, the characteristics of love, and the uniqueness and permanence of love.

In almost every endeavor of life, there is an indispensable ingredient. If you bake a cake and omit the shortening, or if you bake rolls and have no yeast, or if you cook meat and forget the salt, an indispensable ingredient is missing. If you plan to become a concert pianist and lack the discipline to practice, no matter what your talent, your dream will not be realized. Paul reminds us that in the Christian life, there is an indispensable ingredient.

Love, Paul writes, is the indispensable ingredient in God's service. Without love, the richest endowment is of no value, as "sounding brass." If you occupy a pulpit, sing in the choir, act as the church treasurer and do not have love, you are as sounding brass; each of us has seen this kind of hollow service.

Lacking love, marvelous gifts avail nothing toward building the kingdom of God and winning the lost. Gifts unaccompanied by love are useless and may even do damage. Organs can be played to impress other organists; sermons can be preached to show wisdom and learning; men can make of the church a forum for mutual admiration or a place to wield power.

You may speak with the eloquence of Demosthenes, preach like Chrysostom, sing like Caruso, but if you have no love, you are a liability to your church. Is intellectual knowledge your gift? Intellectual attainment can become snobbery or intellectual Pharisaism. The cold contempt of the learned man can repel and destroy others not so endowed. Even passionate faith is not enough. Faith can be cruel. The Crusaders had faith, but they butchered until blood ran in the streets when they took Jerusalem, even rejecting cries for mercy. The Inquisitors had faith, but they thought it was necessary for men to live and die in "The Church" to be saved, and they used torture, even death, to force people to accept their way.

"Although I bestow all my goods to feed the poor . . . and have not love . . ." To give as a duty or with contempt is not love. Such giving brings humiliation to the recipient.

Henry Drummond said, "It is very easy to toss a copper to a beggar on the street; it is generally an easier thing than not to do it. Yet love is just as often in the withholding. We purchase relief from the sympathetic feelings aroused by the spectacle of misery. It is too cheap, too cheap for us and often too dear for the beggar. If we really loved him we would either do more for him or less." [3]

You remember Oliver Twist asking for more. What he really wanted was not more gruel, but more love. He could have lived without the one; he could hardly exist without the other. It is love that makes a gift of value in the sight of God! Don't ever forget that! Even martyrdom may be sought from sub-Christian motives and without genuine love.

After verse one there is not one descriptive adjective used in the Greek text. Paul employs verbs, for love is dynamic and active, never static. Interestingly, the New Testament is given to verbs and not adjectives. The question of who God is, is answered by what he does. It is the acts of God, and not his qualities, that hold the center of the stage. We are told what Jesus did. Paul gives no definition of love. He simply tells us what love does. There are two affirmatives, eight negatives, and finally, four positives. No one has ever translated it better than Dr. Moffatt:

> Love is very patient, very kind.
> Love knows no envy.
> Love is no braggart.
> Love is not inflated with its own importance.

Love does not behave unseemly.
Love does not insist upon its own rights.
Love is not easily exasperated.
Love holds no grudges.
Love is never glad when others go wrong.
Love is gladdened by goodness.
Love is always eager to believe the best.
Love is always hopeful.
Love never disappears.[4]

Tertullian, an early church leader, stood in awe of Jesus, declaring that men should have known he was God because of his infinite patience. You see, Tertullian was petulant, irascible, and quick-tempered.

The proverb on the old castle wall where Martin Luther spent that eventful year reads:

> I love a thing that's fine
> Ev'n when it is not mine,
> And, though it never mine can be,
> Yet it delights and gladdens me.

Thomas Aquinas defined envy as "sadness at another's good." There is no cure for envy but love in the heart. When Lord Byron's poems first came out, an anonymous reviewer enthusiastically praised them, and declared that "in the presence of such products of genius, Sir Walter Scott could no longer be considered the leading poet of his day."[5] It was afterwards discovered that the anonymous reviewer was Sir Walter himself. "Love is not easily irritated." "Love is long-suffering."

George Eliot in *Daniel Deronda* says, "Those who

trust us educate us." It is love-believing! And it is love that redeems us. The minister who loves his flock cannot spend his time in flattering his flock.

Love never disappears, never fails, never falls down on the job. George Herbert wrote: "Such love is like seasoned timber; it never gives way." Love never disappears! It is of eternal value! Love never fails, but leads on to the wholeness which is God himself. Love both brings maturity and reflects it. Love is unique and permanent.

Do you recall that touching story of Leo Tolstoy's, "Where Love Is, There God Is Also"? In the story he tells of Martin Avdeich, the old shoemaker, who lived in the basement. His wife died and left him with one boy who was the joy of his life. He had intended to let the boy go live with a sister, but he could never bring himself to do it.

However, there came a day when the boy sickened and died, and the old man was disconsolate. Finally, a friend came to see Avdeich and reminded him that he was in despair because he was trying to live for his own happiness instead of God's.

"But how can one live for the sake of God?" Martin asked.

"Read the Bible," his friend advised, so Martin began to read the New Testament, often until late in the night. One day he read that remarkable passage which contains the promise, "Inasmuch as ye have done it unto one of the least of these, my brethren, ye have done it unto me." That night he dreamed that Jesus would come to visit him the next day. He awoke with keen excitement, and while he had certain misgivings, he went to work expectantly. He saw an old soldier, recognized him by his shoes, and invited him in for tea when the old man became weary. Then there was the young mother and the child whom he helped; and the old apple lady and the boy trying to steal her apples (whom Martin succeeded in reconciling).

He went to bed that night disappointed because Christ had not come, only in his sleep to hear a voice say, "Martin, did you not recognize me?" He discovered that in each of the three, Christ had come. The old man had learned that where love is, there God is also.

Everybody wants to be loved, and everybody, I suspect, wants to have a lovable personality to which people respond. But love, like happiness, is not achieved by frontal assault. To seek it for yourself is to miss it. To extend it toward others is to see it grow in your heart. Your personality changes since the more you love others, the more lovable you yourself tend to become. Such always begins by focusing on others rather than yourself.

But how can we love like that? How can we focus on the needs of others? How can we care for our neighbors and our enemies as we do ourselves? When threatened, it is natural to retaliate; self-defense is a primal human instinct. Love is what Paul discovered in God's revelation in Christ Jesus. It is Jesus' love that makes our love divine. And we love him because he first loved us. It is God's love for us that frees us from self-centered preoccupation with being loved, and makes it possible for us to begin the process of focusing on others' needs.

One of the ironies of history lies in the fact that sometimes nonbelievers, even the enemies of the faith, have understood it better than some who have accepted it. Consider Celsus, that brilliant Platonist, man of the world, and early critic of the faith, who lived in the second century. He once said scornfully, "These Christians love each other even before they are acquainted." He was scandalized by Christianity's concern for what he called "the rag-tag of society." He wrote: "The root of Christianity is its excessive valuation of the human soul, and the absurd idea that God takes an interest in man." But the thing that astonished him beyond measure was the idea that God, transcendent and ineffable, had descended to dwell among men and submitted himself to the shame of Calvary. It scandalized him, it affronted him, it ran counter to everything he had been taught and believed. It was God's *agape* in Christ that Celsus could not accept—his humiliation, his suffering, his death.

Now Celsus must be given his due. He was a brilliant, candid, honest, outspoken pagan. He rejected the gospel of Jesus Christ, and he did it without apology. But at least he understood what he was rejecting.

It was this love of God for man that filled the first believers with such astonishing joy. For Paul it was the source of ceaseless wonder . . . how he, who had been a persecutor of the church, could be called to be an apostle. John Newton, the wayward sea captain and slave trader who became the hymn writer, used to say, "Can God convert the sinner? Look at me!" A few weeks before he died he said to a visitor, "My memory is nearly gone; but I remember two things: I am a great sinner, and Christ is a great Saviour!"

Our love for others begins in His love for us!

3. Love Is Patience

"Nobody will know what you mean by saying 'God is love' unless you act it as well."

—Lawrence Pearsall Jacks

"Dear God, I pray for patience. And I want it right now!" Oren Arnold calls it the prayer of the modern American. Patience is not our stock in trade, yet this is where Paul begins when he tells us what love does. "Love is very patient, very kind." Or as J. B. Phillips translates it, "This love of which I speak is slow to lose patience—it looks for a way of being constructive." Frankly, without 1 Corinthians 13, I would never have thought of putting patience first in speaking of love; yet there it is. If we are to love, we must learn to be patient.

Patience is not one of my striking virtues. Growing up in the Depression years, work was a law of my home. Indolence is difficult for me to tolerate. I believe life was meant for living, and a person is to pursue his own happiness, strive to be independent and mature.

It is hard for me to be patient with those in the church who view the congregation in terms of "what they do for me." I find it difficult to wait until committees have studied every facet of a problem before they decide what to do. I have to remind myself frequently that "love is *very* patient, *very* kind." And I have to

33

remind myself of all the patience and kindness that has been showered on me through the years—parents who loved and believed that I would mature, churches who forgave the mistakes I made, especially in those early years when I knew so little about pastoring a flock, and always the patience of God.

Sometimes I think that the very degree of our caring as believers permeates our work with an urgency that makes us impatient. The fact that I want the best for you may tempt me to press unduly and to become impatient. All parents understand this. But patience is disciplined care, controlled concern.

Have you noticed that patience is the first and last word of Paul's central verses? *"Love is patient; love is kind* and envies no one. Love is never boastful, nor conceited, nor rude; never selfish, not quick to take offense. Love keeps no score of wrongs; does not gloat over other men's sins, but delights in the truth. There is nothing love cannot face; *there is no limit to its faith, its hope, and its endurance"* (NEB).

In defining what love does, Paul begins and ends with patience as the proof and test of love. This patience is not some stoic resignation, nor the determination to keep a stiff upper lip despite life's pain and tragedy. Paul is declaring that love can take all life brings, stand up under strain, and always act the same.

"Very kind" breathes the quality of God himself. The Old Testament word *hessed*—lovingkindness, grace— is kin to this. It is a positive consideration that is neither discouraged by the failure of others nor embittered by the caprice of untoward events. Love may be clever, but never at the expense of kindness and consideration. Continued kindness flourishes in the soil of patience.

Impatience erodes kindness, good manners, and courtesy. Lacking patience, can a man demonstrate continuing goodwill?

How does a person learn patience? For most of us, it has to be cultivated; people are rarely born with it. Some of us seem to come with an innate intuition and capacity for patience due to biochemistry. Some acquire it unconsciously through the nurture of a Christian rearing. For many of us, it is acquired through years of discipline and surrender to God's will in our lives.

The Bible speaks at length about patience. In Exodus 14:13, we read, "Fear ye not, stand still, and see the salvation of the Lord." Or "Sit still, my daughter, until thou know how the matter will fall" (Ruth 3:18). In Isaiah 40:31 we read, "But they that wait upon the Lord shall renew their strength."

Paul wrote in Romans 5:3, "We glory in tribulations also: knowing that tribulation worketh patience." But not always. James said, "Knowing this, that the trying of your faith worketh patience. But let patience have her perfect work, that ye may be perfect and entire, wanting nothing" (Jas. 1:3,4). Trouble and testing can teach patience but not necessarily. Tribulation may embitter, make cynical, destroy. Sooner or later every man's faith is tried. Such times reveal the health and integrity of a man's faith yet no man would choose them simply to learn patience. It is one thing to talk about the "patience of Job" and quite another to learn to practice such patience.

A somewhat exasperated friend once said, "The best way to learn patience is to work for the government or to enlist in the armed services. If the routine and

delays don't drive you crazy, you've got it made!"
Henry Ward Beecher concluded, "There is no such
thing as preaching patience into people unless the sermon is so long they have to practice it while they hear."
He believed patience can only be learned in the hurly-
burly of life.

Patience is closely related to gratitude. It is also kin
to forgiveness. The only people who can forgive others
are those who know they have been forgiven. Patience
begins in grace, God's grace and man's resultant gra-
ciousness. Since I am aware of God's patience with
men and his great mercy toward me, I can be patient
with his other children. Knowing I err, fall, sin by diso-
beying my Lord, I must have patience with my brother
whose fragile nature is like my own. The person devoid
of gratitude sees no reason for exercising patience toward other people. Learn thanksgiving if you would
learn patience.

Patience also has to do with confidence in God. If
we believe God holds the final word, the ultimates of
our lives, we can wait. If we know "He's got the whole
world in his hand, you and me in his hand," we can
wait with patience. You recall the oft-told story of the
little girl who peels back the petals of the rosebud and
explains she is helping God bloom the rose, and Mary
Riley Smith's little poem, "God's Plan":

If we could push ajar the gates of life
And stand within, and all God's workings see,
We could interpret all this doubt and strife,
And for each mystery could find a key
But not today. Then be content, poor heart!
God's plan, like lilies pure and white, unfold:

We must not tear the close-shut leaves apart—
Time will reveal the calyxes of gold.

Life's mystery and our limited knowledge make patience a necessity. And it is in patience that we find our soul's and God's power.

When I am sore beset I seek some quiet place,
Some lonely room or barren, windswept hill,
And there in silence wait alone until
I see again the smile upon God's face.

I feel his presence fill me like the dawn
And hear once more his whispered, "Peace, be still,"
And know again the strength to do his will.
I turn and take my load and find it gone.

—Antoinette Goetschius

The patient know they're loved and God's love is the final reality. George Matheson, the blind hymn writer, expressed it well:

O Love that wilt not let me go,
I rest my weary soul in thee;
I give thee back the life I owe,
That in thine ocean-depths its flow
May richer, fuller be.

Patience is closely related to one's goal. Michelangelo called genius "eternal patience," and we moderns say "an infinite capacity for taking pains" is the best substitute for genius. It was because Michelangelo's goal was so awesome, so worthy that he gave himself to such

infinite perfection and detail. Patience is a necessary
ingredient, not only of genius, but of all excellence.
"He that has patience," said Franklin, "can have what
he will." And Horace Bushnell declared, "The greatest
and sublimest power is often simple patience."

But the excellent craftsman is not always a patient
friend. The artist is not always the best wife or mother
or husband. Patience in craft, skill, or profession does
not always carry over into human relationships.

If you were asked to name the greatest portrait paint-
ers of the eighteenth century, you might select Joshua
Reynolds and Thomas Gainsborough. But there was
a third, less famous and destined to more obscurity.
He was George Romney, son of poverty, who grew
up in England without schooling after the age of
twelve, and worked in his father's carpentry shop until
he was nineteen.

At twenty-two he fell seriously ill; recovering, he
married his nurse. Soon restless, he left her to seek
his fortune. He saw her only twice in the next thirty-
seven years, but he sent her part of his earnings. In
1782 he painted a portrait of Lady Sutherland, for
which he received eighteen pounds (recently it sold
for $250,000). In 1799, broken in body and mind, he
returned to his wife; she nursed him again as she had
done forty-four years before. He lingered through
three years of paralysis and died in 1802. His wife's
patience and kindness may be more unique and beautiful than any picture her husband ever painted.

And patience is the soil out of which kindness grows.
John Wesley's father once asked his wife, "How could
you have the patience to tell that blockhead the same

thing twenty times over?" "Why," she replied, "if I had told him but nineteen times I should have lost all my labor." To what degree was John Wesley's astounding ministry attributable to his mother's patience? Perhaps herein lies the genius of parenthood. Sharing in patience for endless years! Planting seeds that grow oh so slowly!

What is the essential element in parental love? If you were to ask me the main quality of those who made love tangible to me in my childhood, I would reply, "patience and kindness." I would call it the Golden Rule of marriage and the home. I wish there could be engraved on every wedding band, "Be kind to one another." The child is to obey the parent, but the parent is to be kind to the child.

In the ancient world, children were much under the domination of their parents. "Patria Potestas," the Roman law of the father's power, gave the parent absolute power over his child. He could even sell him into slavery; he could make him work as a farm laborer; he had the right to condemn his child to death—and to carry out the execution. All the rights belonged to the parent, all the duties to the child. And in our day there is widespread child abuse.

The New Testament sets a different standard. There is mutual obligation and responsibility. And love not only involves our children, but our enemies as well. How easy it is to be stringent in our demands and negligent in our encouragement! Mary Lamb, essayist Charles Lamb's sister, finally became mentally incompetent. She would ask, "Why is it that I never seemed to be able to do anything to please my mother?" Or

that poignant statement of John Newton: "I know my
father loved me—but he did not seem to wish me to
see it."

Martin Luther's father was so stern with him that
Martin found it difficult all his days to pray, "Our Father, who art in heaven." To Luther the term *father*
suggested severity and hardness. In reflecting on his
own experience, Martin Luther used to say, "Spare
the rod and spoil the child. It is true. But beside the
rod keep an apple to give him when he does well."
The carols he sang, the stories he told, the games he
played with his own children were a corrective contrast
to his own childhood. Henry Drummond once observed, "The greatest thing a man can do for his heavenly Father is to be kind to some of his other children."

John Boyle O'Reilly expresses the same truth in his
poem, "What Is Good?"

> "What is really Good?"
> I asked in musing mood.
>
> Order, said the law court;
> Knowledge, said the school;
> Truth, said the wise man;
> Pleasure, said the fool;
> Love, said a maiden;
> Beauty, said a page;
> Freedom, said the dreamer;
> Home, said a sage;
> Fame, said the soldier;
> Equity, the seer;—
>
> Spake my heart full sadly,
> "The answer is not here."

> Then within my bosom
> Softly this I heard:
> "Each heart holds the secret;
> Kindness is the word."

Do you desire "the more excellent way"? Then practice, "Love is very patient, very kind." Anyone can practice kindness—its ministry can be achieved by all men, rich and poor, learned and illiterate. Each of us has received kindnesses. Sometimes it is a smile, a friendly look, a simple act such as picking up the conversation when we flounder, a silence when we cannot bear to talk. Does not every person need kindness?

We most often think of kindness as the way one speaks, and the Bible talks of the tongue and kindness, "In her tongue was the law of kindness." Though the writer is speaking about the attributes of wisdom, surely each of us would like to be known as a person in whose "tongue is the law of kindness." It was William Wordsworth who said, "That best portion of a good man's life, his little, nameless, unremembered acts of kindness and of love."

> Have you had a kindness shown?
>   Pass it on;
> 'Twas not given for thee alone,
>   Pass it on;
> Let it travel down the years,
> Let it wipe another's tears,
> 'Til in Heaven the deed appears,
>   Pass it on.
>
> *—Henry Burton*

4. Love Is Optimism

"What we love we shall grow to resemble."

—Bernard of Clairvaux

David J. Schwartz in *The Magic of Thinking Big* writes: "Our six-year-old son, David, felt mighty big when he was graduated from kindergarten. I asked him what he planned to be when he finished growing up. Davey looked at me intently for a moment and then answered, 'Dad, I want to be a professor.' 'A Professor? A Professor of what?' I asked. 'Well, Dad,' he replied, 'I think I want to be a Professor of Happiness.' " [1]

Robert J. McCracken tells of a man who developed his catering business into a successful chain of restaurants. As he lay dying his relatives gathered around his bed. They bent over to hear his final words. His last whisper was, "Slice the ham thin."

There you have at least two different attitudes toward life. And there is widsom in the naïvete of the child. How different life would be if all of us were Professors of Happiness! There is enough frustration, defeat, and sorrow without magnifying it. (As one of my friends says, "There's enough bigotry without organizing it.")

We live in a time when optimism is a suspect word.

43

Man's superficial confidence in progress has given way to a mood of pessimism and despair. One reason for this is the reaction to the sentimental dreaming of the Gay 90's, the "war to end all wars" of World War I, and the flippant optimism of the Roaring 20's, plus the research-computerized promises that came to possess us during the 50's and 60's. Many of these dreams have gone largely unrealized.

The smoke of Hiroshima and Nagasaki still hangs like a cloud over men's minds; the trauma of Vietnam; fighting in Northern Ireland and the Mideast; the violence of our cities; the credibility gap in our institutions; the persistance of cancer; and the imperfectibility of human nature haunt our aspirations. Thinking men have been profoundly affected by the philosophers of pessimism: Kierkegaard, Nietzsche, Ibsen, Schopenhauer, Kafka, Sartre—gifted and brilliant men who have laid bare the disorder, chaos, cruelty, callousness, and tragedy of our human existence. Many have concluded this was the predominant thread of our time, but it is not. Pessimism never tells the great part, for our Lord said, "Be of good cheer, I have overcome the world!" In the world, there is defeat, violence, hopelessness, sorrow, and despair, but there is also goodness, truth, hope, faith, and love. Love is stronger than hate, hope outlasts defeat and despair, goodness is more prevalent than violence though we hear more of violence, and faith faces death with optimism for faith looks forward to a new tomorrow. God is still in his heaven despite evidence that not all is right with the world. He holds the scales and they are weighted on the side of faith, hope, love. Give yourself to them

and never fear, come what may. They are the ultimates.

What is the optimism of love? "An optimist," an un-
known sage has said, "is the kind of person who believes
a housefly is looking for a way to get out."

Do you recall the story of the three men who are
sitting at the counter for a cup of coffee? When the
coffee is served, the cream is out of reach. The pessimist
says, "Pass the pitcher." The realist says, "Pass the
milk," and the optimist says, "Pass the cream."

"I am an optimist," Winston Churchill once observed. "It does not seem to make much use being
anything else." Helen Keller's comment is perceptive:
"Keep your face to the sunshine and you cannot see
the shadows."

That kind of attitude is the best kind of all! Pessimism
requires neither courage, daring, nor faith. Any man
can expect and await the worst. The cynic has really
excused himself from involvement. To choose optimism is to choose hope as a way of life.

The Bible is a book of optimism, not sentimentality
or Pollyannaism. No book is more candid, honest, and
realistic. Yet no book is as hopeful, reassuring, filled
with promise. And the basis of biblical optimism is
God's love made tangible in Jesus Christ. It is God's
love that cleanses, forgives, heals, releases, makes free,
reconciles, redeems, gives assurance and hope.

There are a thousand texts to confirm the truth of
biblical optimism:

Genesis 1:31: "God saw every thing that he had
made, and, behold, it was very good."

John 1:12: "But as many as received him, to them
gave he power to become the sons of God, even
to them that believe on his name."

John 3:16: "For God so loved the world, that he
gave his only begotten Son, that whosoever be-
lieveth in him should not perish, but have everlasting life."

Matthew 28:18,20: "All power is given unto me
in heaven and in earth . . . and, lo, I am with
you alway, even unto the end of the world."

2 Corinthians 5:17: "Therefore if any man be in
Christ, he is a new creature: old things are passed
away; behold, all things are become new."

Philippians 4:13: "I can do all things through Christ
which strengtheneth me."

1 John 4:16: "And we have known and believed
the love that God hath to us. God is love; and
he that dwelleth in love dwelleth in God, and
God in him."

This is optimism in its noblest and most vital sense.
To discover the love of God is to find meaning and
purpose in life—and the motivation and resources for
living a new kind of life. The optimism of love entails
many things: confidence in God's grace and power,
the assurance of my own value and worth, an awareness
of the potential in every human being, a posture of
encouragement rather than criticism, and an acceptance of the power of an endless life.

I am an optimist, not because I act like one—for
many times I do not—not because I believe in the inev-
itability of human progress or that the human race
will eliminate war, poverty, injustice, and inequality.

Not because men will solve all their problems through economics, education, politics, sociological schemes, or the perfectability of human nature, but because I believe the God of this universe is a God of love who has made this love available in Jesus Christ, redemptive and reconciling. The optimism of love rests firmly upon the loving action of God in Jesus Christ. And he is calling men, not only onward, but upward. The optimism of love is not optimism in general, which often is little more than faith in faith or the power of positive thinking. The believer is optimistic about human nature because he has experienced the love of God in Jesus Christ.

No biblical text better characterizes the optimism of love than 1 Corinthians 13:5-7. "Love holds no grudges, takes no pleasure in other men's sin, rejoices in the truth" (Author). Moffatt has a beautiful translation at this point: "Love is always eager to believe the best." Of course! I remember a person of whom it was said, "Even his mother had trouble believing in him!" He was in bad shape! A pulpit committee chairman once told me that a certain pastor had been recommended to the committee by his mother! Wives, sweethearts, fathers, mothers, friends—thank God for the optimism of love!

Sometimes we say, "Love is blind," but this is an enormous generalization. Real love sees and is the most perceptive of all.

"Apparently she sees something in him nobody else does!" Of course, and in seeing it, she helps bring it out. To love all is to make all good things possible. Love is full of faith, hope, and expectancy. My confidence in you is nourished by my love for you. "Love is always eager to believe the best!" The reason for love's hopefulness is not hard to find, for God is love. Have faith in God, and you cannot reject love. In him all things are possible!

You remember when your parent came to see you, and you introduced that parent to a friend, and the friend complimented you. Your parent couldn't let the matter rest but added other good qualities. Embarrassed, you protested gently: "Aw, Mother!" Yet all of us know, deep inside, the miracle of being so loved is one of life's precious treasures. Who can say what degree of our progress is a direct result of such loving by someone? Paul knew this kind of love and said, "Love bears, believes, hopes, endures all things." He knew that our human loves are but reflections of the divine love. As Barrett has said: "Love supports the world."

"Love bears all things, believes all things, hopes all things, endures all things." Paul speaks no longer about what love is not, but about what love *does*. Love can endure the strain, take it on the chin, stand without faltering, meet any emergency. But what is more, love bears, believes, hopes, endures when it comes to life's choices, priorities, and relationships. Love alone sees persons as they really are. It discovers the best and brings it out, and it is God's key to human redemption. Love never gives up. Love is the reality that overcomes everything that would defeat and destroy man. Four times in verse seven Paul uses the word "all." Love can bear any insult, injury, provocation, disappointment. This can read, "Love covers all things." Love believes all things; love is completely trusting. Love takes God at his word. Love believes the best about the other person and this brings out the best in that person.

When Dr. Arnold became headmaster at Rugby, he instituted a new way of doing things. Prior to his coming, school had been terror and tyranny. He called the boys together and advised them they were free *on their honor*, but that they were responsible to act as gentlemen. The boys found it difficult to believe and even more difficult to accept. When they were brought before him, they continued to make old excuses and tell old lies.

"Boys," he would say, "if you say so, it must be true— I believe your word." They were astonished. But as a result, there came a time when Rugby boys began to say, "It's a shame to tell Arnold a lie—he always believes you!" He believed in them, and he made them what he believed them to be. The time came when they spoke the truth and behaved as gentlemen.

Love never ceases to hope! Ask a mother about her boy in prison, or a devoted wife about a wandering husband. It is love's nature to keep on hoping to the very end.

George Matheson, a blind hymn writer who lost his sight and the girl he dearly loved, wrote in one of his prayers for the acceptance of God's will, "Not with dumb resignation but with holy joy; not only with the absence of murmur but with a song of praise!"

The optimism of love prevails even in the trauma of death. Arthur John Gossit, a renowned clergyman, told of the anguished days immediately following his beloved wife's death. His first sermon after her death began with these lines: "In the night of death, hope sees a star; and listening love hears the rustle of a wing."

It was listening love that heard the angels' Laudemus
Te at Jesus' birth. Even in death there is the optimism
of love.

Love declares: you can change human nature, men
can turn around, alienation can be overcome, brotherhood is a possibility, men can learn to care for each
other, peace is a reasonable goal, life can be made better because God's love is available in Jesus Christ! That
is the optimism of love!

Aren't you glad that the measure of our usefulness
to God is not that of our faults and failures? Nowhere
is this seen more vividly than in the life of the man
who wrote the second Gospel. Mark has been called
the Gospel of youth because of its pungency, brevity,
directness, and power.

Who was this man, Mark? He was the son of Mary,
a well-to-do woman of Jerusalem, whose house became
a meeting-place for the early church. From the beginning he was brought up in the center of the Christian
fellowship. He must have been a gifted, impetuous,
indulged, and somewhat self-centered young man.

When Paul and Barnabas set out on their first missionary journey, they carried him with them. Upon
reaching Perga, Paul proposed to strike inland. When
Paul did so, the young man's resolution failed, and he
left the expedition for home. We are not sure why
he became a turncoat. Perhaps fear, the hardships
ahead, some petty disagreement, or the desire for return to the comfort of an overprotective mother.

Paul and Barnabas completed their first journey and
then planned to set out on a second. Barnabas, who
was Mary's brother and therefore Mark's uncle, was
anxious to take the young man again, but Paul refused

to have anything to do with a turncoat.

So serious was the difference between Paul and Barnabas that they split company, never again working together. Barnabas took the young man with him on a separate missionary journey.

In this haunting and disturbing story, there is much we do not know, but we do know that this young man reappears in the most surprising manner. To our surprise, when Paul writes his letter to the Colossians from prison in Rome, Mark is with him. And when Paul is waiting for death and near the end, he writes to Timothy, saying, "Find Mark and bring him with you; for he is useful to me" (2 Tim. 4:11). It is a far cry from the day when Paul would have nothing to do with Mark because he was a quitter.

Whatever happened, this young man had earned the title of "the man who had redeemed himself." It is interesting that he was the one who was qualified to transmit Peter's gospel to the world. Likely it was his Uncle Barnabas, called specifically "the son of encouragement," who was the key to the redemption of this young man. Mark is a vivid illustration of the optimistic power of love. It is the optimism of love that can transform a quitter into an evangelist.

5. Love Is Maturity

"Love is simply the name for the desire and pursuit of the whole."

—Aristophanes

Carl Binger once tried to portray the meaning of maturity. Picture in your mind an eighteen-month-old infant suddenly grown to a six-foot tall, 190-pound man.

But in all other respects he has not altered. He drools, spills his food, screams, wrecks the house when irritated, and, when it suits his fancy, becomes a monstrous menace. Now imagine that during his period of rapid growth, his intellect develops proportionately. He is bright, clever, quick. He has a degree from a great university in business, law, or medicine. But he has no concern for the feelings or welfare of others. He uses people and becomes infuriated when people protest or rebel. He is impatient, overbearing, self-centered, peevish.

Now such a man might well become the president of a corporation, but pity his subordinates and the members of his family. Or perhaps even more logically, a member of Congress. He might know nothing about government or care about the concerns of ordinary citizens, but he would be a go-getter and a vote-getter. His politics would not be constrained either by ethics or good taste. Conflict of interests would not disturb him. Compromise would be his middle name.

You see, the first infant turns out to be a physical menace and the second, a moral one. And yet no evil has been added to them. They are as people like to say, "little boys at heart." Psychologists tell us that the tragedy of the world is there have never been enough mature people in the right place at the right time.

Maturity! Did you think about it as a dimension of love? Maturity is not considered an exciting virtue. Most of us sense that it is costly and demanding, involving more than we want to give. All of us admire and appreciate it in others, especially in those we must live with. We expect it of our parents, demand it of our doctors, lawyers, and pastors, but can be lenient toward ourselves. Maturity in those who love us is a trait we desire, but sometimes we imagine we can love others adequately without maturing ourselves.

One hurdle we have to overcome in our pilgrimage toward maturity is our citing of immaturity in others. We do well to remember that each of us has an amazing ability to rationalize our actions at the time we are doing them. My course of action may seem reasonable to me; actually, my action may appear glaringly immature to an observer. So it is with the other person. Talking about other people's immaturities, just contemplating them, may make for pleasant diversion. This may lead to gossip, scintillating humor, "respectable" blackmail, but no good comes, and great harm may be committed. It is best to settle some things within ourselves. Let's concentrate on our own immaturities. Let's be realistic and practical, facing our faults but not overwhelmed by them.

Paul's negatives in 1 Corinthians 13:4-7 describe the

most elevated and positive values in the world. Why did Paul use a series of negatives? Because love is so contrary to our normal human pattern? Or because love was so untypical of the Corinthians' behavior? Perhaps it was because love was rarely exhibited in the first-century world. Or it may be that jealousy, arrogance, resentment, vengeance, revenge, and rudeness are so familiar, Paul used them in contrast to the very opposite, love.

No man can live the life of love and fail to do what love does. In verses 4-7, the characteristics of love are defined; in strong verbs, this passage tells us what love does. "Love is very patient, very kind," and we search our souls in context of love's patience. Paul makes eight statements as he defines love. Each is a mosaic in the winsome portrait of the mature person.

> Love is very patient, very kind. Love knows no jealousy; love makes no parade, gives itself no airs, is never rude, never selfish, never irritated, never resentful; love is never glad when others go wrong (author's composite translation).

Many people have tried to define maturity. A fan wrote Dear Abby and asked her to define maturity. Her response has merit: "Maturity is the ability to do the job without being supervised; finish what you begin; carry money without spending it; bear an injustice without wanting to get even." But this definition falls far short of Paul's proofs and tests of *agape* love.

Note the specific traits that complete the portrait. "Love knows no envy." Some wag has said there are only two classes of people in the world, "those who

are millionaires and those who would like to be." The
envy that covets and the envy that resents are akin.
"Love knows no envy."

Along with most ministers, there was a time when
I could have said that no parishioner had ever confessed
jealousy to me. Then one Sunday morning, a handsome
ten-year-old boy sidled into the door of my study and
softly said, "I have a problem." I invited him to sit in
a chair near my desk where we could talk. This charm-
ing boy looked straight into my eyes and said, "My
problem is, I am jealous of my little brother." I was
tempted to throw my arms around him and shout, "My
young friend, you are one in a million!" How perceptive and brave he was! We don't confess jealousy, I
think, because we are ashamed to admit it; it makes
us seem so little.

People are of equal worth before the throne of God.
But here on earth, we have to grapple with the inequi-
ties that are a part of our human heritage. In native
endowment, position, success, we are so unequal. Even
more haunting, some of these inequalities are forever
irremedial. What justice is there in one child's having
an I.Q. of 160 and another an I.Q. of 80? One man is
born to excessive wealth and another to poverty.
Haven't each felt the pangs of envy? There is only
one cure for envy, and that is the love of God in the
human heart. Truly mature is the person who can, with
patient sincerity, rejoice in the greater success of another in a sphere aligned to his own. Only Christian
love is pure and strong enough to endure the differences in endowment, status, and circumstances which
are a part of our human lot. And love alone is pure
and strong enough to make gracious and grateful those
generously endowed.

"Love makes no parade, gives itself no airs, is never rude. Love is no braggart." Envy is an inward state of the soul. Boastfulness is the outward expression of the insecure person. Love is neither conceited nor overbearing nor puffed up (a balloon full of hot air). Love does not recite a catalog of its virtues, its freedom, its accomplishments. Some people confer their love as if they were conferring a favor. Real love is like unto God's—it gives without thought of recompense.

Genuine love never gets over the wonder of being loved and from that gratitude comes humility. Love is not inflated with its own importance.

William Carey was one of the world's geniuses. He went out to India despite the opposition of the East India Company and the elitist power structure prevalent in the England of his day. He became a great linguist, supervising the translation of the Bible, or parts of it, into thirty-four dialects. He became a botanist of world renown and the founder of William Carey College at Serampore.

At a dinner in Calcutta, one of the guests leaned toward Carey, then famous, and said, "I believe, Mr. Carey, you were once a shoemaker."

"No, your lordship," replied Carey, "just a cobbler." Love "gives itself no airs . . . is no braggart."

Love is not selfish. It does not insist upon its own rights. All men have a propensity for one of two attitudes: to think in terms of their rights or to think in terms of their duty. Some men think, "Life owes me such a thing," and some men pray, "Lord, what can I give?" Love lives to give, not to receive.

Love is never irritable. No statement is more all-encompassing or more demanding. Love never loses its cool, becomes exasperated, loses its balance. Here again is the ring of patience. No doubt it is closely related to the "peace that passeth understanding." Someone has wisely pointed out that love can be irritated without being irritable. There is today so much that should irritate a Christian, and complacent unconcern would be a sin of vast proportions. Love is marked by the maturity that evinces itself in balance, serenity, and even temper.

Love does not store up the memory of any wrong that it has received. The word translated "store up" is an accountant's word. It is the word used for entering an item in a ledger so it will not be forgotten. Yet this is precisely what many of us do. Learning what to forget is one of the great arts in life. Love does not keep track of all the wrongs received, brood over slights, or cherish resentment. Remember to select your memories; make them those which nourish the Spirit of God in you.

Love is never glad when others go wrong. A strange, sad fact about human nature is that men often take pleasure in other men's misfortunes. Sometimes like wild animals, when a man is down, others will crowd in for the kill. Pure Christian love has no malice, no brutality, no sadism. Christian love is kind. To take pleasure in the failure and misdeeds of others is to reveal a malignant heart.

There is something awesome about Paul's word a bit later: "When I was a child, I talked like a child, I thought like a child, I argued like a child; now that I am a man, I am done with childish ways." Love means growing up. When I was a child, I fell from a footlog across a creek and broke my left arm. That night was one of excruciating, persistent pain.

I thought I couldn't bear it until my mother brought her cot and lay down beside me. It was the maturity of her love that sustained me in my anguish and fear. She was steady, dependable, patient, kind, and understanding. The long hours of that night passed more quickly because she was there. Love not only wants the best—it gives the best. It thinks, talks, acts as a child no more, for it has put away childish things. Full-grown people can meet the demands of the *agape* lifestyle. A childish person can receive love, but only a mature one can give it, and persons need to love even more than to be loved. The unloved are pathetic, but the loveless, those unable to love, are deprived and handicapped.

Maybe there is no such thing as maturity, only the process of maturing. We are all in process, we are becomers in pilgrimage, and we grow in community. A psychologist tells of the man who came to his office to have his wife "repaired." Complaining of her immaturity and her inefficiency as a wife and mother, he asked the psychologist what could be done for her.

"I'm an engineer," he explained, "and when something goes wrong, I go to someone who can fix it. I've had my wife sent to four doctors, and all of them concur that there is nothing physically wrong with her. So I decided to bring her to you. Fix her! I'll pay whatever it costs."

The psychologist invited *him* to remain for therapy, but he refused. As a result the case proved hopeless, and the woman later committed suicide. Parents often bring children to psychiatrists, insisting that they cure their children without touching the parents' problems.

Do you remember our Lord's words in the parable

of the talents? "Well done, thou good and faithful ser-
vant: thou hast been faithful over a few things, I will
make thee ruler over many things: enter thou into
the joy of thy Lord" (Matt. 25:21). I guess you would
call that an abundant entrance into eternity. Recall
the words of the apostle Paul in Ephesians 4:13: "Till
we all come . . . unto a perfect man, unto the measure
of the stature of the fulness of Christ." These magnifi-
cent texts suggest that those who stand high in eternity
will be those who have grown in the maturity of love.

Most of our distinctions here on earth are artificial
and repugnant to God. What is God's kind of person?
The Bible answers in a variety of ways: He has "clean
hands and a pure heart" (v. 4), and has not lifted up
his soul unto vanity, nor sworn deceitfully, we learn
in Psalm 24. In Proverbs 31 we are told that the woman
after God's own heart is industrious, productive, trust-
worthy, and that "strength and honor are her clothing"
(v. 25), and "in her tongue is the law of kindness"
(v. 26). The prophet Micah declares that God requires
three things of all men: "To do justly, and to love
mercy, and to walk humbly with thy God" (Mic. 6:8).
Don't these qualities describe the maturity of love?

A friend of ours died the other day. I have written
of her before. She was old when we met her nearly
fourteen years ago. She was a plain little woman, unob-
trusive, devoid of pomposity, but alive and compassionate. Her loyalty, generosity, concern for others, gaiety,
humor impressed us as the years went by. Impressing
others was not her style; she preferred action to talk.
She never made headlines, received any legacies, or
was given any special privileges. For forty years, she
was a high school science teacher. She was a gold-star

mother with one living physician son far away in Canada. Retirement freed her to live the kind of life she had always wanted to live. She was in the "Keenagers," alright, but always serving rather than being served.

I remember when she came by my study with a check for the church building fund. "I didn't come to get attention," she said somewhat apologetically as she handed me the envelope. "I wanted to let you know we'll finish the job." She saw my chin drop when I discovered the size of the check. The check was for $5,000. She lived in a $12,000 house and drove a ten-year-old economy model car. With a twinkle in her eye she said, "You've been looking at my car. I like to give my money to things that don't depreciate."

I have thought about her in the last few days. She managed to escape the booby traps of old age: the sun-porch of nostalgia, the bedroom of complaint, the living-room of self-pity, the corridor of senility, the family-room of peevishness. She neither whined nor advised nor berated. She felt no compulsion to boast of either her virtues or vices. To her, action was preferable to conversation, kindness to criticism, and humor to despair. And when she died, she left her last $30,000 to the church she had loved so dearly. She gave her life to things that don't depreciate.

If there are ranks in heaven, she'll have a high place, although I know she'd be irritated at me for saying so. The reason is simple. She had grown full-measure "unto the measure of the stature of the fulness of Christ" (Eph. 4:13). She possessed the maturity of love. Only the full-grown can love in the spirit of Christ.

6. Love Is Energy

"Love will find a way."

—English Proverb

Love is energy, a fact often ignored but biblically true. What greater force is there in the universe? We Christians believe this truth deep in our hearts, give lip service to it, but too infrequently practice it. Living in a power-conscious age, we neglect the greatest power of all.

Energy has always fascinated man. He has been awed by the surging tide, learned to respect the force of gravity, both feared and worshiped the energy of the sun, exulted and cowed down before the power of the wind. Today he has developed a new energy vocabulary of words such as fossil, solar, nuclear, thermal. He is no less dependent on the energy of the earth than was his most primitive ancestor.

Physical energy is a necessity, inescapable and urgent. But the energy of love is more urgent. Why do we think so often only in terms of physical energy—economic, military, political forces which coerce, manipulate, and even destroy—and neglect the energy that cleanses, heals, restores? The energy of love is miracle-working, life-changing, and joy-giving. The energy of love is the Christian's weapon for waging God's warfare in the world.

There are manifold reasons for our neglecting the energy of love. We fail to comprehend love as energy. We persist in the incomplete view of love as merely passion, sentiment, or abstraction. Humanity has always known the force and pleasure of sexuality. It is an integral part of biological survival. But biblical love is other than and more than sexual passion. And we have always tended to sentimentalize love. We make it a golden dream, a romantic story, a trip into wishful thinking. A concept so limited is enough to thwart countless marriages. Nothing demands realistic love more than marriage; those who marry soon discern this. Clergymen and professors have often been guilty of making love an abstraction, something we endlessly talk about, spin wonderful theories upon, and make as practical as gossamer.

Love is often confused with pity which sees a need, rings its hands, and feels badly. And love has many counterfeits. One is love-*talk*, a doctrine exalted as a virtue and often the subject of sermons. Whether in our conversation or our theology, love is more than talk. There is the counterfeit of mere sentiment; love is often confused with the mere *feeling* of love. And all this leads to the conceiving of love as a beautiful abstraction.

Sinclair Lewis in his satire about clergymen, *Elmer Gantry,* reports how that hypocritical preacher plagiarized on Robert Ingersoll by using the famous agnostic's words about love: "Love is the only bow on life's dark cloud. It is the Morning and the Evening Star. It shines upon the cradle of the babe and sheds its radiance upon the quiet tomb. It is the mother of Art, inspirer of poet, patriot and philosopher." [1] There is resonance and beauty and truth in these words, but they inadequately present love. In the New Testament, love goes beyond sentiment, beauty, wistful yearning; it almost always encompasses a deed. Love is coupled with loving action. It works in vigorous ways to help people. It shares, cares, and even dies to redeem.

The study of energy fields is basic in modern science.[2] Pioneered by men like Michael Faraday and James Clark Maxwell, it has produced our ingenious electronic technology and our worldwide communication network. By observing variations within energy fields, we have been able to follow the development of the most distant galaxies and the pulsations within the very heart of the atom. Energy fields are an integral part of all forms of organic life.

If you sprinkle fine sand on the sounding box of a violin and draw the bow once lightly over one of the strings, the energy field produced by the vibrations will arrange the sand in a variety of patterns such as a square, a triangle, an ellipse, or even a snowflake-like pattern of symmetry and loveliness. The same sort of interaction between particles and an energy field can be demonstrated by placing a magnet under a surface covered with iron particles. The magnetic field, acting on all particles simultaneously, will arrange them in geometric forms.

In like manner love is energy which creates patterns of beauty and meaning in the lives of human beings. And just to think of love as energy serves as a corrective to many false views.

"Love is the medicine for the healing of the world." [3]

This was the conclusion of Dr. Karl Menninger, the psychiatrist, in *Love Against Hate* (1959). Today his conviction is even stronger:

> There are many people in the world who are neither our patients nor our students, and who are nonetheless filled with great apprehensiveness, partly from ignorance and mistrust of one another. They are afflicted with great suffering which all our discoveries have not ameliorated, and awed by vast discoveries which none of us fully comprehend.
>
> . . . .
>
> For these people—for them and for ourselves— are we not now duty bound to speak up as scientists, not about a new rocket or a new fuel or a new bomb or a new gas, but about this ancient but rediscovered truth, the validity of Hope in human development—Hope alongside of its immortal sisters, Faith and Love.[4]

7. Love Is Permanent

"To love abundantly is to live abundantly, and to love forever is to live forever."

—Anonymous

Out in New Mexico there is a town and tribe of Pueblo Indians named Acoma, which may be the oldest inhabited settlement in the United States. The settlement is strikingly situated atop a mesa rising 350 feet above the surrounding plain.

Many students of anthropology have speculated as to why the Acoma built their dwellings atop the mesa. Willa Cather in her provocative novel, *Death Comes to the Archbishop*, debates the matter. There may be, she suggests, a number of reasons: one, for instance, would be security. Rising high above the plains with restricted access, the mesa was easy to defend. Then there were the natural cisterns with their bountiful water supply. Food and water could be crucial, especially in times of drought. But the primary reason was their hunger for permanence. The great rock mesa was solid, strong, enduring. Just to live on it gave them a sense of continuity. And all men hunger for permanence.

Repeatedly the Holy Scriptures speak of it. Take Psalm 90, "Lord, thou hast been our dwelling place in all generations. Before the mountains were brought forth, or ever thou hast formed the earth and the world, even from everlasting to everlasting, thou art God." Those are the first two verses. Now notice verse four: "For a thousand years in thy sight are but as yesterday when it is past, and as a watch in the night." Or the last two verses, "Let thy work appear unto thy servants, and thy glory unto their children. And let the beauty of the Lord our God be upon us: and establish thou the work of our hands upon us; yea, the work of our hands establish thou it." Or Hebrews 13:8, "Jesus Christ, the same yesterday, and today, and for ever." He is the "eternal contemporary," "Jesu, joy of man's desiring," both now and forever.

Yet so many things are temporary. Men have always searched for the permanent. They have amassed wealth, purchased property, struggled for power, run for political office, strained for professional excellence, constructed grotesque and monumental mausoleums. They write books, paint pictures, build buildings, organize governments, always hoping men will remember them. Yet fame at best is a fragile thing, a capricious mistress with limited favors and intense anguish.

In 1 Corinthians 13:8-13, Paul declares that the permanence of God is embodied in the permanence of love. It is love that endures, never fails, understands, perceives, matures, abides. The whole sequence dramatizes the permanence of love:

"Love never fails"
"For we know in part"
"When I was a child"
"For now we see through a glass darkly"

"And now abideth"
"But the greatest of these"

I have thought about the comments of an aged man
who had gone back to visit his childhood home after
an absence of more than sixty years: "Nothing was the
same. The schoolhouse had been torn down, the church
rebuilt, and a shopping center constructed where the
old home place used to be. My friends and neighbors
were gone, and everything seemed so strange. The
years make a difference, don't they?" He sat pensively
for a moment, and then abruptly added, "Everything
was changed except one; my only brother loved me
still!" Love lasts!

When the mountains have been ground to dust, the
evermoving tide ceases to move, and the changing sea-
sons stop changing, then love, *agape*—God's love for
man and man's love for God and his fellowman—shall
remain fresh, young, and vibrant through the endless
ages of eternity. If you want to build on that which
endures, follow after love!

In verses 8-13 Paul has three final things to say about
Christian love. First, he stresses its absolute permanence. When all the things men glory and pride themselves in have passed away, love will still stand. Fashions and styles, whims and moods, human taste and
preference, that which impresses and entertains—
these things come and go, but love endures. The poet
was so right:

The mind has a thousand eyes,
The heart but one;

Yet the light of the whole life dies
When love is done.

There is an old Latin proverb: "A man is not where
he lives, but where he loves." And John Greenleaf
Whittier knew his Bible when he wrote:

Life is ever Lord of Death
And love can never lose its own.

Precisely, because "where love is, there is God also."
To give one's life to temporary, transient values such
as money, prestige, power, possessions, pleasure is to
pauperize it. These things are alright in their place,
but they are means and not ends. Men share the fate
of those things they give themselves to. A life of love
is a heavenly treasure, more precious than all the
wealth on earth.

There is a lovely text in the Song of Solomon: "Many
waters cannot quench love, neither can the floods
drown it" (8:7). Love is the one unconquerable thing.
This is one of the reasons for believing in life after
death. When love is entered into, there comes into
life a quality and a relationship against which the as-
saults of time are helpless, and which transcend the
process of death itself. Michelangelo's sense of propor-
tion, Keat's love of beauty, Beethoven's perception of
melody, Francis of Assisi's awareness of joy and faith—
these things are timeless, for death has no hold on
them. Love is like that, for within its truth lies the
power of an endless life. Did you ever sit and listen
to a seventy-year-old talk about the wife or husband
or child who died forty years ago? The relationship is

just as real, as vibrant, as precious as it was years ago. This stands in sharp contrast to the fashions and styles of fifty years ago which today seem a triviality and an amusement, while love is still pure and precious.

If you question the premise, then sometimes sit down and study Paul's reasoning in Romans 8 where he delineates the love of God which nothing can separate us from. "Neither life nor death, neither messengers from heaven nor rulers on earth, neither what happens today nor what happens tomorrow, neither power from above nor power from below, nor anything else in God's whole world can separate us from the love of God in Christ Jesus our Lord!" (Rom. 8:38,39). Or 1 John 2:17, "And the world passeth away, and the lust thereof: but he that doeth the will of God abideth for ever." And the life of love is the will of God.

Next Paul stresses the absolute completeness of love. The verse is an interesting one: "For now we see in a mirror dimly, but then face to face. Now I know in part; then I shall understand fully, even as I have been fully understood." It is in the context of love that we understand ourselves and others. Without love knowledge is always inadequate and partial. Even the scientist searching for a cancer cure must love his work, or else he will not give it the careful attention necessary. This is true of the musician, the artist, the technician, even the bird-watcher, and it is certainly true of understanding another human being.

Human personality is so complex, paradoxical, ambiguous that no man can really understand another human being if he does not care for him and love him. Most students of literature (while recognizing the flaws of adulation and sentimentality in the writing of biogra-

phy) would agree that few authors can really succeed
in telling the story of another person whom they do
not admire—simply because love is necessary for genuine understanding of another personality. In the context of love we must learn to understand.

Corinth was a center for the manufacture of mirrors,
and Corinthian mirrors were the best in the world.
Despite that fact, they were dim and imperfect; for
in that day mirrors were made of silver and bronze.
It would be a particularly vivid metaphor for the people who received the letter. So it is, Paul points out,
with man's understanding of God and life and eternity.
We sense a God of beauty, order, love, and truth, yet
there is so much to baffle us—violence, suffering, evil,
confusion. Man does not understand. He tries to con-
vince himself, to trust and believe that his life is set
in the middle of a friendly universe, but sees as in a
mirror dimly. Man's understanding of God is always
partial. In fact, the rabbis had a saying that it was
through a mirror dimly that Moses saw God. This was
reflected in the exclamation of Job, "Oh that I knew
where I might find him!" In his life Paul felt all he
had been able to see, at best, was a reflection of God—
that is, until Jesus came, and in God's love made tangible Paul had come to see God in reality and truth.

The mystery, of course, is on man's side, not on God's.
Even if in Christ we have the perfect revelation, our
seeking minds can grasp it only in part, for the finite
can never grasp the infinite. Our knowledge is still
like the knowledge of a child. But the way of love
will lead us on until that day when we know as we
are known. We cannot ever reach that day without
love, for God is love, and only he who loves can see
God.

Finally, Paul stresses love's absolute supremacy. There are three things that live on: faith, hope, and love. They embody the awesome strength of God, the values that endure, the virtues that stand the strain, bear the burden, make the difference. But why does Paul declare that love is the greatest of these? Why is love reckoned superior to the other two? One observer observed that faith without love is cold, and hope without love is grim. Love is the fire which kindles faith, and love is the light which turns hope into certainty.

Is love reckoned superior because of its wider application? There are times when faith is almost nonexistent in the human heart and when hope becomes despair. All of us have experienced this in hours of anguish and turmoil when we have had to struggle to hang onto credibility and expectation. In such times love is all we have left. Indeed, love is the only one of the three which everybody can do. There is never a time when I cannot love somebody. Paul declares that even the most favored and gifted cannot live without it, and yet it lies within the reach of the poorest and most limited.

John Eliot was a grand old missionary to the American Indian. He was sensitive to and loved the American Indian when almost no one else did, to the point of translating the Bible into the Indian's language. As an old man, worn out and ill, conscious of his failing faculties, he confessed: "My understanding leaves me, my memory fails me, my utterance fails me; but I thank God my love holds out still."

Long centuries ago Erasmus wrote: "Paul writing to the Corinthians sets love higher than miracles and prophecy and tongues of angels. Never tell me that love consists in going often to church, kneeling before shrines of saints, lighting candles, and multiplying rosaries. God has no need of such practices. Paul calls it love to edify your neighbors, to count them all members of the same body."

Love is wider in application, but it is also more lasting. It endures. When diamonds have turned to dust and gold is no longer of value, then men will see love for what it really it. (Why do you think the streets in heaven are paved with gold?) There will come a time when automobiles, houses, lands, stocks, bonds, hard cash, fleshly appetites no longer have meaning; then love will be the very essence of existence. It lasts on when faith and hope have little meaning and purpose.

Love is also nobler in scope. It embraces and encompasses faith and hope, and is the foundation upon which they are built. Faith and hope so-called can be used for selfish ends. But love by its very nature cannot, or it is not love. Our love for others is an extension of God's love. Dr. Phillips in his translation of John's epistles speaks of our showing "a strong family likeness to Jesus." We do this by the practice of Christian love.

And finally, love is reckoned superior because it is the essence of God's nature and his weapon for the redemption of the race. To know a God who is love we must learn to love. Faith and hope can be a private exercise for our own edification; Christian love relates us to others and God, and is directed outside ourselves. And love is God's power for making men new. Love works when nothing else will. It not only outlasts the others; it outperforms them. He who knew all possible alternatives chose the way of love.

I believe the most powerful energy on earth is love's

energy. It is the miracle-worker, the life-changer, the joy-giver, the great healer. As someone asks, "If we do not love others, how can we help them?" There is a beautiful parable told of a couple who lost an only son in World War II. The experience, of course, was heart-rending, and they thought they could not bear it. One evening in desperation they prayed, "Oh God, we feel we cannot bear it unless we are granted the privilege of seeing him once more for five minutes."

According to the parable an angel appeared granting their request, with the stipulation that they specify which five minutes in their boy's life it would be. Would they prefer to see him as an infant in arms, or the first day he went away to school, or when he graduated from the university with honors, or the day he went away to service, or when he chose to give his life so heroically?

Finally, the parents concluded that they would prefer the day when, as a little boy, he came in from the garden, tearfully asking their forgiveness for some childish wrong. In that moment the temporary was encompassed by the eternal, making vivid the meaning of love. Even in the night of death, "hope sees a star and listening love hears the rustle of an angel's wing." The hope of the world lies in harnessing the energy of love.

Teilhard de Chardin, that remarkable French Jesuit, brilliant paleontologist, philosopher, and Christian mystic, saw sin as the failure of love. He said before he died, "Some day after we have mastered the wind, the waves, the tides and gravity, we will harness the energy of love: then for the second time in the history of the world, man will have discovered fire!" [1]

8. Love Is Choice

"Love is love's own reward."

—John Dryden

He was an old man, soft-spoken and even whimsical. I met him once while visiting in a little church. I guess you would call him a "country philosopher." Perhaps "quaint" is the adjective. "When you get right down to it," he observed, "all the best things: generosity, usefulness, happiness, love—are matters of choice. Nobody decides but you."

The years have confirmed what the old man said long ago. Neither circumstance, nor chance, nor fortune, nor favor make life sweet and satisfying. Whatever difference I can make is determined by my choice.

And love begins with choice. To follow Jesus is to live the life of love, however inconvenient, demanding, or painful. How can a God who is love be served in other than a loving manner? To love will likely bring gladness, but not necessarily. Indeed, as all of us know, to love can bring pain, anguish, frustration. But if we are to be disciples of Jesus, we must live lovingly. This is a choice everyone must make. Some refuse to love because they are afraid. With others it's an unwillingness to be inconvenienced. With some it is reluctance to be made vulnerable, and with others it is innate

hostility which they are either unwilling or unable to
conquer. Hostility and love cannot live in the same
heart; one will eradicate the other. But if we mean
to love we must get at it, for learning to love is like
learning to swim—you can't do it without taking the
plunge.

There is no better example of both the price and
the choice entailed in love than the living experience
of Corrie ten Boom, who barely escaped with her life
from a Nazi concentration camp. Have you read her
little book *Prison Letters?* During World War II as the
German armies rolled over most of Europe, crushing
countries in their path, Adolph Hitler set in operation
a plan to exterminate all Jews. Many people in Holland
responded by doing their utmost to help Dutch Jews
escape. Corrie's father, who was 84 at the time, and
his family engaged in that dangerous enterprise. When
warned he would say, "I am too old for prison life,
but if that should happen, then it would be, for me,
an honor to give my life for God's ancient people, the
Jews." [1] Then there came the day when thirty-five
members of the family and friends were arrested and
carried away. That night the aged father asked his son
to read Psalm 91, and then he prayed. His prayer was
grounded in promises such as:

"He that dwelleth in the secret place of the most
High shall abide under the shadow of the Al-
mighty" (Ps. 91:1).

"I will say of the Lord, He is my refuge and my
fortress: my God; in him will I trust" (Ps. 91:2).

"He shall cover thee with his feathers, and under his wings shalt thou trust; his truth shall be thy shield and buckler" (Ps. 91:4). Corrie was imprisoned and subsequently moved to two concentration camps, the last being the notorious Ravensbruck. Her father and her sister died in concentration camps, and Corrie was miraculously released just one week before all women her age and older were to be put to death. The release was a result of a mix-up in serial numbers.

The letters are poignant, haunting, astonishing. "How greatly prison deprives people of the most elementary conditions of life." [2] "I sing inside nearly all day long." [3] "Time is something to be waded through." [4]

"God did not let his sovereignty slip through His fingers." [5] "I was free and I knew then as I know now it was my chance to take to the world God's message of the victory of Jesus Christ in the midst of the deepest evil of man." [6]

Corrie ten Boom chose to love even those who imprisoned her and destroyed her family. During her confinement days she resolved if she lived to be free she would return to Germany one day to tell of God's forgiving love.

After being released from prison she felt the need to write one final letter—to the person who had betrayed her family's work for the Jews to the Nazi authorities. There are lines in that letter dated Haarlem, June 19, 1945, which in light of the agony this betrayer had brought to the ten Boom family carry a degree of forgiving love that only God could make possible:

The harm you planned was turned into good for
me by God. I came nearer to Him . . . I have
prayed for you, that the Lord may accept you
if you repent . . . I have forgiven you everything. God will also forgive . . . if you ask him
. . . Jesus is standing with His arms apread out
to receive you.[7]

Christian love is by nature volitional. We choose to
love God. We choose to love our friends, our family,
our associates, our fellow church members. We choose
to love those who dislike us, those who mistreat us,
even those who hate us. And finally, we choose to love
ourselves.

Let us be candid with ourselves. To choose to love
is not a decision that can be made on the basis of self-
interest, logic, or personal satisfaction. The person who
lives by the law of love may indeed end up getting
the short end of the stick. From the perspective of
many people in our world, Corrie ten Boom did. But
love is God's way and incidentally the only way which
leads to eternal life. Love is alive now and forever.

Christian love is love by choice, love motivated by
the will and implemented by action and conduct. You
may not like me. I may bring you no pleasant feelings;
there even may be something about me that causes
you displeasure. However, if you love me with Christian love you refuse to act other than for my good.
Christian love is "to have the mind in us which was
in Jesus Christ." [8] Now this kind of love is unique to
the Christian faith and while it can be painful and difficult to live by, it is revolutionary in its power to heal.
And ultimately this kind of love brings the kind of

joy the world neither gives nor takes away.

How do we make the choice? How do we learn to love? Love is both a gift and an achievement—something given and something claimed. Historically, love has been approached in a variety of ways.

There is the symbol of *the ladder of love*. Here we begin where we are with the nearest and the lowest object of love and ascend a step at a time to the highest and worthiest object of love. There is considerable truth in the symbol, for this is what occurs in the development of the human being from infancy to old age. If growth is healthy and normal the circle of love is ever-widening. Yet, experience indicates that one step does not automatically lead to another. Many people seem to get hooked at different levels and never move on. Take the difference between a Casanova and a Francis of Assisi. There are both values and dangers involved with the concept of the ladder of love.

Then there is *the leap of love*. This is a mystical approach where we begin with the highest rather than the lowest. Many of us discovered God's love in Jesus Christ early and it was so enervating, exhilarating, and liberating that it made us want to love everybody—including ourselves. There are multiplied instances of this in the New Testament and in the hymnal. But even the leap of love requires patient and sometimes painful development, application, and maturation.

The essential problem in how to love lies in the ordering of our loves. The Bible does not say, like so many of our contemporary self-help books, "Thou shalt love thyself with all thy heart, and with all thy soul, and with all thy mind, and with all thy strength. . . . And next thou shalt love thy neighbor, and at last, with whatever energy thou hast left, thou shalt love God."

The Bible is realistic about human nature and takes for granted that most of us tend to do a good job of loving ourselves. The real problem is ordering our loves. When our loves are disordered a schism is created in the soul. The proverb, "Your time is your life," relates directly to our loves. Our use of time is determined by our priorities. We decide what we love by what we do, and we decide what we do by how we use our time.

Yes, love is choice. We *choose* to love. And remember, we begin both with loving God and ourselves. Healthy self-love is what God intends. Accept your humanity and be glad about it. Bear in mind the old Persian proverb: "There is no saint without a past; no sinner without a future."

Exercise the faith which God has planted in you and believe in a God of love. Start with his love for you. Remember the Bible says that while no man has seen God at any time, those who love each other know him. Love confirms itself, for to give love is to receive it in return. And perhaps nothing is sweeter than to see the fruits of our love in the lives of others. The chief reward of love comes from the fact that love is the law of our being. To love is to be able to love again . . . and for this purpose we were created.

9. Rerouting Our Loves

"Where there is sorrow, there is holy ground."

—Oscar Wilde

"We were happily married for forty-four years and he went without a moment's notice. It isn't easy to redirect one's love." It was the heart-rending confession of a dear friend who lost her husband. Many of you know what she meant.

Love is the most powerful force in the world, the energy of God at work in the lives of men. Yet love, when it is blocked, can give the most devastating heartache, the most excruciating pain.

Sooner or later even our noblest aspirations must be modified to conform to life's realities. You intended to be a doctor, a lawyer, a nurse, a preacher, or an artist, but had to change your plans. You set your heart on a reasonable and worthy goal which was, you thought, to the best interest of all, and a twist of circumstances checkmated the whole project. You missed your best opportunity perhaps through no fault of your own. You experienced a business failure or the loss of a job. You were suddenly confronted with a deep sorrow, the death of a loved one, the disgrace of a child, the blight of hope, an unwanted divorce.

All of us know there are times when we have to

reroute our plans. We dream our dreams, set our goals, carefully nourish our hopes, but life compels us to make adjustments. But our loves are much harder to reroute than our plans. There is a sense in which all dreams have to be adjusted, and love can only be absolute in intent.

The Buddhists have a moving way of adorning the graves of their dead loved ones. We visited the famous "Punchbowl Cemetery" while in Honolulu and saw famous war correspondent Ernie Pyle's grave. But we noted especially the flowers and fruit on the Buddhist graves. One young Buddhist husband and father, whose young wife and two small children were killed in an automobile accident, would come to the cemetery each week. He would carefully place china, silver, flowers, and food for four on the grave of his wife and children.

Consider, for example, the couple with the Mongoloid infant. In their days of agony, they try to reconstruct the sequence by which their child became a reality. They remember the exhilaration of growing affection in marriage and the anticipation of parenthood. Then there was the waiting after pregnancy, and finally, the day of delivery. It slowly dawned on them that the child they had borne could never share in the normal interchange of love.

The separation caused by death is painful, but the separation caused by divorce can be even more painful. In addition to the void caused by loneliness, there is the remorse that comes with a sense of failure and the pain because it often involves rejected love. This can do terrible damage to one's self-esteem. Many a person hastens to remarry to reassure himself that he is lovable.

One of my friends contends that when it comes to rerouting love after the loss of a spouse, men have fewer problems than women. She explains: "Take Charlie Chaplin, Pablo Casals, Aristotle Onassis, and Justice Douglas, for example. A man can easily remarry; often a woman cannot."

There is considerable truth in the observation that remarriage is more probable for men, especially when they are famous, wealthy, or both. Our culture tends to place a decreasing value on women as they pass beyond their so-called "beauty-years," a vicious sort of sex discrimination.

But when it comes to frustration and loneliness, men appear to be more vulnerable, less able to cope, following the death of, or separation from, a spouse.

In some form, it is likely that sometime each of us will have to cope with painful adjustments. And a part of that coping will be the ability to reroute our lives. Each has to contend with different adjustments. Sometimes it's relatively simple, sometimes not.

A family moves to a new city, and the parents have to adjust to new friends, new church, new work; a child has to leave school friends and the familiar home and build new friendships. The readjustment is unsettling, even traumatic, as it takes months to make new friends and feel at home. Some psychologists define love as attachment and our attachments have to be rerouted.

It is far more difficult to reroute our personal loves. The last child leaves home, an only child marries, and (especially if the child is male in our culture) he may largely be surrendered to the new daughter-in-law's family. Some parents tell how they never again had their son at home for Christmas or holidays.

In a real sense, our lives must be redirected when we retire. This is especially true for men, for many men identify their own worth and esteem with the success of their work. Work becomes their life. If they truly love the profession they have pursued for years, it is urgent upon retirement that this love of work be redirected. They must find another way to use their skill or profession through volunteer work, a hobby, or a craft. Countless retirees are now becoming mission volunteers within our homeland or overseas, giving a definite period of time in service within a hospital or school, or as a builder of churches, or as a teacher. Work becomes a gift that gives blessing to the recipients and blessing to the giver.

The most painful readjustments of all are those that come after separation, sorrow, rejection, or tragedy involving those we love. The death of a husband or wife, a parent or child is beyond all words to describe. These losses are wrenching and final, and life is always diminished afterwards. But maybe hardest of all to bear is the heartache and tragedy involved in wayward or shameful acts of a loved one. Such often disgrace a family.

In one of my pastorates, there was a lovely family who had a severely handicapped son in his thirties. The family was fine, caring people who had borne their sorrow with grace and courage from his infancy. This grace and courage was reflected in the happy disposition of the afflicted son. One day a prominent woman said to the mother, "It must be the worst tragedy of all to have such a retarded and crippled son."

The mother thought a moment and said quietly, "It has been the great sorrow of our lives, but, no, I don't think it is the most dreadful or tragic thing that can occur to parents. For me, the most dreadful thing would be to have a son who grew up and wasted his life and was in the penitentiary."

Sorrows have their graduations and degrees of anguish, but David's lament of old, "My son, my son Absalom, would that I had died for thee," is among the saddest that ring out in our land. Many modern parents have been so baffled and bewildered by the life-style of their sons and daughters.

Life's possibilities for being hurt in love are limitless, precisely because to love is to be vulnerable. Many must come to terms with what they will do with hurt. You love someone devotedly, but he or she does not return your love. You loved a child and lost him, perhaps the most tragic of all bereavements. Or you want desperately to enter a professional career but find it impossible. Sometimes our noblest dreams and ideals are blocked, and we have to reroute our love.

When Paul says love is a way—and it is the best way of all—he does not say it is the easiest way of all. Love is not easy to practice on any level. It is easier to hate when confronted by hostility, rejection, or controversy. It is easier to denounce the ills of our crime-ridden cities. It is easier to sit by our fires than to leave a comfortable home and enter the ghetto, or tend the sick, or seek out the hostile person and love him, or to be a missionary in heartbreaking Bangladesh. It is easier to talk about the terrible teenage crime than to love a wayward youth.

Love is not easy to practice all the time even in the home; it is not always easy to use the soft answer that turns away wrath, or to turn the other cheek, or to go the second mile, or to go the way of the cross, but *love against hate* is the name of the game for the Christian.

Some never give themselves in unreserved caring for another because such caring makes them vulnerable to hurt, rejection, heartbreak. It is because you love your child so dearly that it hurts so much if he does wrong. It is because you care so much that it hurts when you fail as you love. It's hard to find the courage to love when you face despair, defeat, ridicule or the unpopular way. The highest courage is to keep on loving in face of despair or failure, knowing it is the best way of all.

How do we reroute our love? Maybe you have read Corrie ten Boom's *The Hiding Place?* For me the gem in that book is spoken by Corrie's father who seems to have been the person of wisdom in her family. You remember she had fallen in love with her brother's classmate at the university, the only such friend she had ever had, and had found joy and wonder. Her brother warned her that his friend might not be serious, but she thought her love was reciprocated.

One day he appeared at her house, and she went to the door. There he stood with a beautiful girl, fashionably dressed, whom he introduced as his fiancée. Corrie managed to get through tea with the family, then fled to her room, and sobbed and sobbed and sobbed. Late in the day, she heard her father climbing the stairs. She thought he would say all those things we parents say at such times such as, "You'll get over it," or, "You'll find someone better," but he said none of those.

He said, "Corrie, do you know what hurts so very

much? It's love. Love is the strongest force in the world, and when it is blocked that means pain." [1]

Then he told her that there are two things we can do: we can kill the love so that it stops hurting, but a part of us dies too; or we can ask God to open up another route for that love. God can give us a way to turn our old human love into perfect love.

As Corrie heard the receding steps of her father on the stairway, she recalled that she was not then able to give perfect love to her friend and his fiancée, but she knew her father spoke truth, and in time she would follow his advice.

She writes, "I was still in kindergarten in these matters of love—he put into my hands the secret that would open far darker rooms than this—places where there was not, on a human level, anything to love at all." [2] During her subsequent years in prison, she was prepared to love in all the dark rooms of the concentration camp.

There is little wonder that even now as an old woman, Corrie ten Boom is able to share with others the wondrous ways of God in matters such as handling separation, getting along with less, security in the midst of insecurity, forgiveness, how God can use weakness, dealing with difficult people, facing death, turning the other cheek, how to love one's enemies, and what to do when evil seems to win.

In her eighties now, Corrie ten Boom is a stout, small woman, vibrant, compassionate, and dynamic. As she speaks, her radiant faith shines through, embodying the love she shares. She bears in her body the marks of the Lord Jesus.

Corrie's father was right—there are two things you

can do with disappointment, frustration, and heartache. You can cut off the feelings for the persons or
circumstance and build a hardness around them to protect yourself, or you can take your blocked love, and
with God's help, make a new dimension in your life.
You can kill the love so it stops hurting, but then a
part of you dies too, or you can ask God to open up
another route for that love, help it mature in accor-
dance with the mind of Christ. Interestingly, it is only
then that we come to know what Paul was speaking
of as "the breadth and length and height and depth
of the love of Christ." [3]

How do we reroute our love? It won't be easy, and
it will take time. There is a time of bewilderment and
shock, when all we can do is simply survive day by
day. But the time comes when we must pick up the
pieces and move on. We are more likely to act ourselves
into a new way of thinking than to think ourselves
into a new way of acting. We must ask God to show
us how to act and begin acting that way. To reroute
love is not to forget or replace the old loves; it is to
learn to live with the loss by giving ourselves to other
loves.

How many childless parents, or those who lost a
child, have let the whole world of children come troop-
ing into their hearts, making them able to give to the
education of countless young men and women, or en-
dow an orphanage, a college, or a children's ward in
a hospital?

How many Corrie ten Booms, denied happy marriage, have rerouted love into teaching the young, min-
istering in faraway places, being the most supportive
person in the life of nieces and nephews? An executive

I know, a woman of great charm and ability, lost her sister when the sister's children were young. This busy, single executive has been surrogate mother and grandmother to her sister's progeny, literally "living in" when there was grave illness, a new baby, or times of stress—supporting, loving, rerouting love for her sister to those whom her sister loved.

And rerouting can mean coming to the place when we love, a perfect love, the one who thwarted our desire. Did someone receive the promotion you desired? Goethe said, "Love is the only defense against superiority." It may be difficult; let us admit it is difficult, to reroute our love, but love finds a way.

God rerouted his love to us. Through the centuries, he sent his prophets again and again to tell us what he is and to guide us. But man would not listen. Finally, he rerouted his love by sending his Son to take on man's condition. This only Son suffered and died patiently, routing God's love by way of the cross.

10. The Miracle of Community

> "To sin is to poison the public reservoir, to love is to strengthen the whole community."
>
> —Leslie Weatherhead

Elizabeth O'Connor in *The New Community* writes: "Persons thrive and grow and come into full existence in relationship with others, and then themselves become makers of community." [1] She vivifies her conclusion by telling of the October when Jennifer Dodge, two years and nine months old, died.

The Christian community (the Church of the Saviour, Washington, D.C.) surrounded the young parents during the surgery (for the removal of the tumor at the stem of the child's brain), during later surgery, and finally death. Elizabeth tells how they gathered in the lovely woodland where the child loved to play and celebrated her life by planting a tiny tree and placing an unbalanced cross the children had made. On that hillside she pointed out how they remembered again and again Jesus' words, "I pray that you may be one, even as I am one with the Father."

Perhaps community comes easier in pain than in pleasure, but it is never a simple matter. People say, "All we have to do is love one another," as if it were easy to do. But it is not. Something within us reaches out for it, and something within us resists it. Genuine community may be the highest achievement of mankind.

"Blest be the tie that binds our hearts in Christian love." That is how the hymn begins. It concludes: "The fellowship of kindred minds is like to that above." To be honest we must admit sometimes our fellowship is less than heavenly. The "fellowship of kindred minds" is not always like that above. At times it seems to point in another direction.

The man who wrote that hymn understood that. His name was John Fawcett, and he spent all of his life in a bleak area of Yorkshire, living in the most strained of circumstances. Left an orphan at twelve, he was apprenticed to a tailor for whom he worked from 6:00 AM to 8:00 PM six days a week. At fifteen he heard George Whitefield preach and was dramatically converted.

Immediately he had a sense of being called of God to the ministry and mentioned the matter to Whitfield who encouraged him. Largely self-educated, he soon found a tiny band of people who encouraged him to "exercise his gifts." The church which resulted was a warm and wonderful fellowship but tiny and made up of the poorest of the poor.

Wainsgate, where he served, was just a cluster of houses, not even a village. Four children were born to the Fawcetts in five years, and when he became desperate, the congregation finally raised his wages to twenty-five pounds a year, but this was mostly paid in porridge and potatoes. Porridge for breakfast and potatoes for lunch and dinner was modest fare. When the prominent Carter's Lane Baptist Church in London called him to be pastor, he felt he must accept if he were to educate his children. The wagons were loaded and the family was prepared to leave. The congregation gathered and began to sing and pray.

Finally Fawcett's wife said to him, "We can't go," and he agreed. As a result John Fawcett lived, worked, and served in the same area for fifty-four years. He understood that "the tie that binds" entails tears as well as smiles, anguish as well as exhilaration. Yet this tie is simply another name for one of the paradoxical wonders of Christianity, the miracle of community.

"We belong to each other!" These were the words of a sixty-year-old woman talking about her childhood family. "There was Dad, quiet, hard-working, firm. He didn't talk much, and sometimes you thought he didn't love you—that is until you got into trouble; then you knew. And Mom, plump and talkative, always warm and generous and helpful, sometimes tired and fussy with an occasional headache, but how she took care of us!

"Then there was Bill, tall and thin and serious. He worked so hard, always obeyed, was nearly always serious, and sometimes would get blue and withdrawn.

"I was next and then Mary. She was pretty, vivacious, witty, popular. She had everything I wished I had, including three dates to my one, and sometimes it hurt. But we were close anyway. With just two girls in the family we had to be to defend our rights. And then there was Bob, bright, confident, adventuresome, and a free spender. He was the baby in the family, and all of us spoiled him. He could get into trouble more quickly and out of it more quickly than anybody I ever knew. I guess you would call him the black sheep and the pet lamb but how we loved him!

"Mom went away ten years ago one Christmas, and

Dad died two years later. He seemed glad to go for
he missed Mom so. And Bob, you know, was killed in
that car wreck last year; he was only thirty-nine. We
were glad it didn't happen until Dad and Mom had
gone, for otherwise it would have killed them. There
are three of us left now, but really there are six—three
in heaven and three on earth.

"You see, we belong to each other!"

In that brief, simple monologue a second daughter
expressed the miracle, the mystery, the wonder of community. John Wesley was right when he said, "No man
can be a Christian alone." In God's plan others must
share the gospel with us if we are to know it at all.
How can we know the love of God except in community? No human being is whole in himself. We were
meant for each other. To live in isolation is not to live
at all. Community is both a spiritual and psychological
necessity.

No miracle is more surprising or comforting than
the miracle of community. To belong to God is to belong to each other. The church is the group expression
of Christian experience. In the community of faith we
come to know a Savior's love; we discover the wonder
of forgiveness; we learn what it means to love and to
be loved; we learn how to reach out to help, to heal,
and to set free. The one characteristic of the early
church that most surprised and impressed the first-century world was the love of believers for each other.
This loving one another was so utterly new in that
world, people found it difficult to comprehend. All persons want to be loved. All sense their need to learn
to love, but much of the world is loveless.

The oldest Baptist church in Kentucky has this in

its records: "It rained so hard we had no preacher so we read a chapter and everybody threw his light as far as it would go."

From the beginning the church has been a sharing of light and love for the healing of humanity. To me a Christian church is, above all, these things: a community of faith, a fellowship of the forgiven, a company of the committed. Or if you please, the family of God.

All these elements are involved in any vibrant Christian fellowship. As believers we share the wonder of forgiveness and a willingness and joyfulness in forgiving. The loving community is to be redemptive in its outreach. This is "the tie that binds our hearts in Christian love. The fellowship of kindred minds" which is "like to that above." Perhaps no congregation ever becomes a real community of faith until it labors, loves, and sacrifices for a common cause. In connection with a church building program, which required huge sacrifices on the part of the members, a young deacon said to me: "We have laughed together, cried together, planned together, prayed together, and agonized together. We have hoped, feared, and even despaired. We have worked, struggled, and sacrificed. We have walked that lonesome valley arm in arm and there have been times when all we have been sure about was Jesus." Belonging grows out of pain and pleasure, struggle and achievement, winning and even losing together.

There is purpose in the hymn writer's words:

We share our mutual woes; Our mutual burdens bear;

And often for each other flows the sympathizing
tear.

It is in such experiences we come to understand what
we have in common: one Lord and one Savior, a common need as sinners and a hope steadfast and sure.

It is important to remember certain truths about
community: *There is power for healing in a community
of love.* A psychiatrist once remarked to me, "If you
church people would really be church in the Christian
sense, you could do what all the psychiatrists on earth
could not do." Then he surprised me with his eloquence and enthusiasm about a loving community's
power to heal. When you contemplate the hurt, cyni-
cism, brokenness, depression, confusion, and rebellion
in each community, you are reminded that the work
of the church is never finished.

Individual wholeness can come only in community.
There are great achievers in the world who are loners.
But to be a loner is to be fragmented.

*The kind of saving that God makes available in Jesus
can only be realized in community.* Love by its very
nature must be shared. To be set free, to care, to belong, to share, to rejoice can only be experienced together.

Death was meant to be experienced in community.
The same could be said about birth, for surely it was
God's purpose that every child be born into a home
of love, and that we move from the church militant
to the church triumphant—from our home on earth
to our home over there—and it is the love of the family
of God that makes bearable the pain of transition and
mystery.

Community lies at the heart of the gospel. Jesus spoke of it often. But what Jesus says is not always what we would expect him to say. "By this shall all men know that ye are my disciples" (John 13:35). What would you normally expect to follow: By how you attend church? By how you pray or read your Bible? By your spirituality? By what you do or what you say, or how you spend your money? By your lack of prejudice, your sobriety, your temperance? By how you treat other people?

But that's not at all what he said. "By this shall all men know that ye are my disciples *if ye love one another.*" It's really a revolutionary concept, contrary to all normal human expectations. How could loving one another change the world? You see, for Jesus every community of believers was the kingdom of God in microcosm. And God's hope for grounding his love and making it effective and powerful to redeem the world. Whenever the church has been a community of love, God's Spirit has come in with mighty power and begun to work miracles. In God's work in the world the ingredients for power are not the same as in our workaday world. Put faith, love, and commitment together in a body of believers and you have the very *dunamis* (power, "dynamite") of God at hand.

We need to remember that this concept of loving one another is not some incidental teaching Jesus expressed at random and soon laid aside. He said: "A new commandment I give unto you, that ye love one another; as I have loved you" (John 13:34). And again in John 15:17: "These things I command you, that ye love one another." As an elderly John wrote: "Beloved, let us love one another: for love is of God; and every

one that loveth is born of God, and knoweth God. He
that loveth not knoweth not God; for God is love" (1
John 4:7,8). Love is the distinguishing mark of the
Christian.

No biblical concept of church is more central or more
heartening than that of the family of God. First, there
is the community that comes because of a common
Lord and Savior. Every member of that body is a forgiven sinner, equally in need, and equally redeemed
by unmerited love. We are brothers and sisters both
in light of our sin and by virtue of God's grace. This
is the basis of our community, and on this ground we
are the family of God.

These fundamental truths result in a radical new concept of stewardship of life and resources. Since what
we have is from God and God is Father of us all, what
we have does not belong to us alone but to others in
their need. Paul's beautiful thought of one's sufficiency
supplying another's insufficiency in 2 Corinthians 8 and
9, is one of the loveliest concepts in all literature.

The first "communism" the world ever knew was
shortly after Pentecost as Acts reports, "They had all
things common." Of course the difference in this kind
of communism and the political communism is radical.
This was voluntary and based upon love. Part of the
reason for the political monstrosity, Marxism, that covers so much of the earth is the fact that so few Christians
have taken this stewardship seriously. Many in the
name of Christ have grown richer and richer while
the masses have grown poorer and poorer.

There is the amazing theology of *koinonía* which
permeates Paul's letters. We translate it "fellowship"
and used to think of it in terms of "dinner on the

grounds" or some sort of jovial camaraderie. In the New Testament, it is miraculous and mysterious and has to do with a tie that binds—the sharing of love, money, and even life itself.

We are a koinonía, a family sealed by God's sacrifice in Jesus, motivated by gratitude and love, a forgiven community which has learned how to forgive. This is central to all that we are and do. And unless we live by it we are not Christ's church at all.

Learning to love one another in community is no simple matter. It is precisely when we are together in community that all of our brokenness is revealed, all of our anxieties and compulsions are laid bare, all of our hostilities and animosities, exposed.

A young preacher who left the ministry once confessed to me, "I have tried, but I never could swing it." Then he quoted this text and added, "There were so many peevish, petty, petulant people in that church that I could never do it. I went into social work and for me it does not seem quite so hard." Perhaps he should have been asked, "Were you never petty, peevish, and petulant yourself?" Congregations have no corner on imperfections.

Remember the story of the small boy who got in a fight with a neighbor boy. His mother found out about it and spanked him. Through his tears he said, "Mama, I would be okay if it weren't for folks." There are times when each of us understands the little boy's feelings. Perhaps we expect too much in the church. When we come to Jesus we bring our failures, faults, foibles, as well as our hopes, dreams, and ideals. The saving process is continuing in our lives. Let us remember it is in community that we find our identity, learn how to belong, and discover what we can do. Apart from community we are always partial, alone, separated.

How can we learn to love each other and subsequently learn to love a world outside? We must keep in mind that community begins with common interests and common commitment. It is what God has done for us in Christ and our response to that miracle of grace that binds us together. Sometimes we sing: "Take the name of Jesus with you, child of sorrow and of woe; it will joy and comfort give you; take it then where'er you go." The name of Jesus brings us together, keeps us together, and is the source of all that we do together.

And we must never forget that community grows in common tasks. To become a part of the Christian family is to take an irrevocable stand. It is like a Christian marriage. It is "till death do us part," with no considerations ever being given to abrogating the contract. Like a good marriage, our relationship to other believers in Christ grows in common tasks. The members of a church down in Birmingham decided to give to a special offering, over and above their regular giving, forty days of their income for the year? That church, with little or no great wealth, raised one million dollars in forty days, and that church became a new fellowship of believers in the process.

Community moves toward fruition when we try to put ourselves in the other person's place. There is a sentence in Mark's Gospel, about Jesus crossing over the Sea of Galilee, which reads: "Let us pass over unto the other side" (Mark 4:35). Jesus was always doing that himself and helping other men to cross over in their thinking and their sympathy as well. He was forever putting himself in the other fellow's place. To worship is to be sensitized toward other people, to be made aware, to see clearer and more completely.

Dr. Robert J. McCracken tells of the Scottish lady, Mrs. MacDuff, who disliked everything her minister did. If he preached a lengthy sermon, it was too long. If he preached a short sermon, it didn't have enough meat in it. If he didn't visit, she said he was aloof. If he did, she said he was trying to win people to himself instead of to the Lord. He could not please her.

He determined nonetheless to include her on his regular visitation schedule. Stopping in front of her apartment one afternoon, he looked up and observed a curtain flutter, indicating that she was watching him. When he knocked at the door, there was no answer. Finally he knelt down and looked through the keyhole only to find Mrs. MacDuff doing the same thing on the other side. He chuckled and said, "Well, Mrs. Mac-Duff, this is the first time we have ever seen eye to eye." Seeing eye to eye requires effort and care. Love which builds community confronts ignorance, deals with prejudice, admits insecurity and fear, and works at understanding.

Turgenev and Tolstoy were walking together down a country lane when they saw an old, broken-down horse standing alone in a field. Tolstoy crawled through the fence and went over to the horse. Putting his hand on the animal's neck he began talking to him. Turgenev said Tolstoy talked with such sympathy and understanding that he thought Tolstoy must have at one time been a horse. That was one of the reasons Tolstoy was a matchless writer. He had learned sympathy for every living creature. Persons who have learned their kinship with all of life begin to lose their fear of life.

It is amazing how different things look from the other side. Take the American Revolution when read from an English history book. It hardly seems to be the same event when you compare it with the orthodox American version. The last time we were in Westminster Abbey, we noted the inscription about the seventeen-year-old English boy who was killed in the Revolutionary War at Yorktown. It read, "Killed October 19, 1781, Yorktown, Colony of Virginia, in American Rebellion." It isn't easy to do what Ezekiel did when he wrote in his prophecy, "I sat where they sat."

To build community anywhere is a worthy and demanding business. In the church, for example, we must be honest about our proclivity for rumor and gossip. We must recognize and admit the inner hostility that so often plagues us. We must learn to work for good, to be peacemakers, to concentrate on the pleasant, the positive, the profitable, and not the negative, the censorious, the destructive. To love another, I must give him the benefit of the doubt. I must learn to forgive him. I must want the best for him. The key words at this point are forgiving, understanding, kind, and supportive.

Community depends on our effort and God's grace. If we love each other, we will work at putting ourselves in each other's places and be prepared for the pain and irritation this may cause. If we love each other, we will accept the fact that however bizarre the other person's actions may appear at the moment, they seem reasonable to him. If we love each other, we will think in terms of potential rather than present limitation. And if we love each other, we will learn how to speak the truth in love, for love's concern is too deep to misrepresent or pervert. If we love each other, we will have discovered the ultimate fruit of God's grace at work in the world. In the glow of that love we will be able to build the bridge of love to a lost world.

In Remarque's famous novel, *All Quiet on the Western Front,* there is an incident about two soldiers in World War I. During a particularly fierce encounter, a German soldier dived into a foxhole, only to find himself lying beside a British soldier. On seeing the enemy uniform, the German instinctively reached for his bayonet. Then he saw that the English soldier had been mortally wounded.

The dying man was fumbling to get something out of the inside pocket of his uniform. Sensing he was in no danger, the German soldier reached over and helped him. The items the English soldier was trying to get were well-worn photographs of two children, a younger woman, and two older people. The German soldier realized that these were photos of the boy's family, and he held them up so the dying man could see them one more time.

The German got out his canteen and wet the feverish lips of the dying man. The English soldier reached out and grasped the hand of the German as he died. It was a poignant reminder that fighting makes men enemies and pain makes them brothers. It dramatically revealed that there is no brotherhood until we get close to one another. Only God's grace can motivate the love that is the mystery and miracle of community.

11. Manners to Love By

"No woman ever falls in love with a man unless she has a better opinion of him than he deserves."

—Ed Howe

"Have you ever thought of putting 1 Corinthians 13 to work in your marriage? The possibilities are endless, you know." She was a soft-spoken forty-year-old woman whose comment came as somewhat a surprise. Her response had been evoked by the painful frustrations which had surfaced in the marriage sharing group. Indeed, at the moment she seemed to be the only one who knew what to say, and it was obvious that she believed it with all her being.

Her suggestion got the group going again on love and what we expect from marriage. As the night wore on it became obvious that many of the married people present were convinced that any individual who marries, expecting a spouse to make him or her happy, is doomed to failure. Indeed it is impossible for one person to make another person happy, for happiness is an inner feeling generated largely by an individual's response to his or her environment. The group finally concluded that the Christian church can be the best friend of the family when it is honest and loving.

Love has been called "the glue of marriage," but on the other hand, it is the glue of all human relationships. When I bring up *manners to love by* I am not referring to marriage alone. The theme is equally addressed to singles, divorcees, parents, children, the young and the old, the rejected and the accepted. All life is in part relationship, and love is not only the glue of relationship, it is the lubricant as well.

Manners to love by! How about yours? Have you kept them in good repair? How would your spouse or your peer or your friend rate you? Are your manners appropriate when it comes to Christian love?

Love is an attitude, a spirit, and a manner of living. The dictionary has a series of definitions: affection, attachment, interest, concern. No doubt the latter comes closest to Christian love for, as we are aware by now, *agape* is unconquerable benevolence and invincible goodwill, which are characteristics of God. And incidentally, there are many times in marriage and any other intimate relationships when nothing but *agape* is sufficient.

If you want to add the Christian dimension to your marriage, your home, your relationship, then measure them by 1 Corinthians 13:4-7. Here is the basis, the maturity, the optimism, the permanence of love. And if I had a text it would be, "Love is very patient, very kind." That may not sound romantic or exciting or startling, but that's the glue of all human relationships, the secret of meaning and purpose in living together.

There is an old saying: "If a child of God marries a child of the devil, the child of God is sure to have trouble with his father-in-law." One is reminded of the scriptural admonition: "Be not unequally yoked together" (2 Cor. 6:14). Life, however, is simply not as pat as the old proverb seems to make it, because no individual is God-like all the time, and no individual is un-God-like all the time.

Marriages may be made in heaven but there's a lot of maintenance work to be done on earth. Someone with tongue in cheek once observed, "God help the man who does not marry until he finds the perfect woman, and God help him still more if he finds her." You recall the good brother who lamented, "The only perfect man I ever knew was my wife's first husband!" There is considerable truth in the old German proverb, "Marriage is Heaven and Hell." Indeed, it is what two people, plus the grace of God, make it.

Manners to love by initially depend, to a large degree, on living in a real world and having emotional and mental health. We bring into marriage what we are, both good and bad, both attractive and unattractive. Marriage is not a reformation society; it may accentuate faults instead of cure them. Further, no marriage is static. We change, interact, influence each other, create our own situations. We make each other better or worse. We are always in the process of becoming. Remember if you don't like what your spouse or friend has become, you probably helped make him or her that way. At least it ought to make you more patient and understanding about it. Frankly, most people expect too much out of marriage or a relationship. We know better, but we persist in imagining that marriage or friendship will transform us as if by magic.

Love is both a gift and an achievement; it must be received and it must be learned. No one deserves either the love of God or the love of a marriage partner or a good friend, but on the other hand if my capacity for love is to be enlarged I must make a deliberate effort to expand, grow, and broaden my perspective. We don't fall in love; we grow in love. In addition, love that endures always has to do with faith. Only God's love can make our love divine.

At this point perhaps it's necessary to remind ourselves that not only did God "earth" his love in Jesus, but our love must come to live in everyday experiences, or it has little validity. Many, for example, have not seen marriage or other binding relationships as a boon. The world has always had its emotional hermits. Simply to read any good book of quotations will make you aware of it.

"Marriage," wrote Menander long ago, "to tell the truth, is an evil but it is a necessary evil."

And Shelley wrote, "A system could not well have been devised more studiously hostile to human happiness than marriage."

And Samuel Johnson wrote, "I believe it will be found that those who marry late are best pleased with their children, and those who marry early, with their partners."

Oscar Wilde was most cynical of all, "Men marry because they're tired; women because they are curious. Both are disappointed."

But remember, marriage is ordained of God and can give life meaning and joy.

One of our principal problems when it comes to expressing love in relationship lies in the assumption that since love is God's gift it comes by magic. Someone has said that marriage takes skill and luck to be successful, skill in communication and enough skill not to spoil the luck. Love and common sense are not enough; we must work at it, and we must work at it lovingly.

Already we have considered the word *love* in our title. Perhaps we should define the word *manners*. Manners is more than wearing a perfect front, handing out a good line, or saying the right thing at the right time. Manners to love by has to do with more than surface relationships. It is easier to seem polite than to feel humane.

Since marriage involves the closest kind of relationship, clever "manner tricks" can prove, not only futile, but emotionally fatal as well. In marriage you cannot pretend love, trust, respect, or companionship; they must be genuine and real or they turn sour. They must be inner and honest.

Marriage is the foundation of the family unit—a unit which no form of society to date has been able to get along without.

You know, of course, there are many reasons for marriage, in addition to a man and a woman's love for each other. Sometimes that is not even the primary one. Reasons such as the desire to have a home of one's own, to find completion of one's self, to settle sexual problems, to have a family, and for the sake of status and security. People marry for wealth, career, opportunity, or social advancement. I am not saying these are necessarily good reasons, just that they are reasons.

When a man and a woman marry they're not just joining two people together. They are linking together the entire effect of their childhood, adolescence, plus their lifetime mental and emotional experiences. In other words, they are mixing together the sum total of their past and all their relationships. How they relate to father and mother, brothers and sisters, home and friends is bound to influence the marriage relationship.

You must be capable of loving yourself before you are able to truly love someone else. This doesn't mean a sort of narcissism, a falling in love with your face when you look in the mirror. It does mean accepting what you look like and making the best of it. It means accepting and liking a whole lot of things about yourself. It means self-awareness.

And unfortunately, as people get older many of them tend to become less and less self-aware, people-aware, world-aware. This leaves their feelings and attitudes frozen. This inside-out dying is undoubtedly mostly due to societal pressures, but it engenders a growing dislike of self and a growing disregard of others. So far as is known, man is the only living creature capable of self-awareness. To really love someone else you have to achieve a relatively solid state of self-identity. Self-awareness leads to "other-awareness" which in turn leads to "together-awareness."

Despite all you learned in mathematics, when it comes to a good marriage one plus one equals far more than a mere two. A happy marriage is not only rewarding to the two parties involved, but to all those around it. In chemistry this one plus one that equals more than two is called synergism. It means that in cases where certain chemicals are combined, each having its own specific reaction capacity, the result of the fusion will be more than double. The combined effect will be far more than the sum of the individual capacities.

The difference between romantic love and married love is the difference between the unreality of the moment and the reality of the duration of time. Or to put it another way, it is the difference between a dream and reality. Earlier I said that loving someone requires the ability to love oneself. Another way of saying this is to state that love for someone else entails a great degree of emotional maturity. Love is a matter of mutual devotion, the willing blending of oneself with another self without fear that one is losing oneself. And love has a way of leaping over all differences that divide.

Two problems in marriage are a sense of disillusionment and the gradual erosion of mannered behavior. "She slurps her coffee and keeps those rollers in her hair." "He throws his clothes around and has those funny bow legs." I guess you would call them unpleasant surprises; they were there all the time, but romance blinded you to their reality.

Life isn't all glamour; you couldn't endure it if it were. And then in anger or frustration one partner injures or cuts the other person's ego, and feeling humiliated, the other person looks for frailties or weaknesses in his or her spouse, and you don't have to look far in any of us to find them. A mature love accepts the frailties of the object of one's love.

All relationships lived in light of 1 Corinthians 13 take on new practicality and new joy. To love is to be realistic about human relationships and not to expect the impossible. Love is enhanced by realism; we love the people who make us feel good about ourselves. This is what Jesus was always doing with people. Like Michelangelo he was forever releasing the imprisoned angel. Honest people are permitted early to feel honest about themselves. Be honest about your emotions. Everybody feels fear. Everybody gets angry. Everybody has trouble with hostility. Don't go around pretending you have never had a nasty thought. Don't tell other people, "We have been married thirty years and never had a cross word." Substitute guidance for criticism. Remember evil is overcome with good. Don't condemn; reward good behavior. If you want beauty in relationship, then make your love tangible.

A single friend complained about this subject, saying, "There you go again, leaving us out!" My response was "Wait a minute. I am including you. You need manners to love by, if for no one else, for that married guy who is always trying to get you married. Why, aren't there times when you would like to tell him where to go and where to stay?" My single friend smiled and replied, "Well, I guess I wanted you to tell him for me!"

One of the special dimensions made available by a God of love is the achievement of better manners to love by, and it's one of the sweetest gifts of the Savior.

12. Love Is Triumph

"We have loved the stars too fondly to be fearful of the night."

Inscription, Allegheny Observatory,
University of Pittsburgh

"What is love?" This is the question we began with and we will end with; an important question any time, an urgent one right now. Has there ever been a generation so in need of love and so obsessed with the desire for it, yet so inclined to pervert it?

We have examined and sought to internalize this love we have found in Jesus. By grace we have chosen to make *agape* our way of life, and despite the partiality of our commitment we have found it revolutionary. Is it possible to express its meaning in a word or in a sentence?

I have asked the question of scores of Christian believers, and the answers have run the gamut. Love is caring. Love is sharing. Love is life. Love is Jesus.

Most people think of love in one of three or four ways. For some it is emotion—the way they feel, and as such, as capricious and ephemeral as a passing moment, great if only it would last. For some it is a belief, a conviction carefully considered and firmly held. Convictions sustain, and to the degree that one can live by beliefs, it is liberating.

For others love is something you do, and while this

is a still better way, the things we do can be motivated by duty or fear and as such, they invalidate *agape*. Increasingly I have come to think of love as sacrifice. Some object to the word *sacrifice* because they have seen it caricatured, a kind of sacrifice that imposes itself on others, as is illustrated by the child who said of his parents, "They are always telling me how much they have sacrificed for me, and I feel so badly about it." But sacrifice in the biblical context has nothing to do with a martyr-type syndrome. It has to do with the joyful offering of the best to God, the laying down of one's own life for the sake of others, the redemptive, healing act which becomes like a fragrance to the Father.

This is the kind of love that the gospel is all about. The Bible is filled with it:

> "For ye know the grace of our Lord Jesus Christ, that, though he was rich, yet for your sakes he became poor, that ye through his poverty might be rich" (2 Cor. 8:9).

> "For he hath made him to be sin for us, who knew no sin; that we might be made the righteousness of God in him" (2 Cor. 5:21).

> "Now ye are clean through the word which I have spoken unto you" (John 15:3).

> "For God so loved the world, that he gave his only begotten Son, that whosoever believeth in him should not perish, but have everlasting life" (John 3:16).

That beautiful expression of God's love in Hebrews 12:2 is intriguing: "Looking unto Jesus the author and finisher of our faith; who for the joy that was set before him endured the cross." Jesus chose to give himself for our redemption, enduring the awful death of the cross for "the joy that was set before him." In the Bible, sacrifice is always for a purpose, never an end in itself. This distinguishes the suffering that is redemptive from suffering that has no meaning, and herein lies a determining distinction when we confront love as sacrifice.

Sooner or later love is sacrifice. This was certainly true of Jesus. Because he loved people so dearly, he had to confront them with their prejudice, hatred, and lovelessness. Confronted people, even those whom we love, do not always adore us. His love involved them at the point of their deepest sin; as a result that very love activated their guilt, anger, and hostility. His own people finally crucified him. One reason those who love are sometimes the persecuted is because such love as Jesus' cannot be casually dismissed. Those who met Jesus could not remain indifferent. Some forces are so great only death can stop them; finally they tried to stop Jesus, even believed they were successful, by the instrument of a common criminal's execution.

Love is sacrifice in parenthood. Most of us enter parenthood thinking of the joys involved, the pride of rearing handsome and bright sons and daughters, the pleasures of familial relationships, and the credit they will bring us. How perfect they will be. Some parents never progress beyond that stage. If children fail to meet their expectations, they become belligerent, hostile, and rejecting. Some parents almost destroy their children by pushing them into these preconceived molds.

For most parents, though, the sacrifice begins early: nights worrying about a baby with colic, anxiety lest he be hurt, the tiredness that comes with around-the-clock care, cancelled parties and trips. For the mature parent, the time comes when love of child involves a willingness for greater sacrifice.

If *agape* measures our relationship, then parenthood commits us to redemptive love, even if perchance in painful, embarrassing circumstance. Have you ever watched a prominent father stand beside a wayward son in court, and, despite the public humiliation and the even greater anxiety for the welfare of the child, let the whole world know that his love has no limits? Love does not count the cost, keep books, or balance the ledger. Love goes to the marketplace, the ghetto, even the cross to redeem that which it loves. Most parents will do anything for the good of their child, even give life itself.

Someone has said that there are three kinds of love: the *if* kind of love, the *because* kind of love, and the *in spite of* kind of love. The *if* kind of love says, "If you are good, Daddy will love you." The *because* kind of love dispenses affection because of something the loved one is or has or does. Some parental love is simply an extension of self-love, and this can be true of children also, as the college kid said to me once, "What I love about my parents is the check from home." But the *in-spite-of* love has no conditions, and it is that kind of love that understands its sacrificial, redemptive nature.

If love begins by way of sacrifice, it ends by way of triumph. The sacrifice is really only a means to an end, and the end is redemption. The price love pays opens the door to the power of a triumphant life. The other side of *love is sacrifice* is *love is triumph*. The Bible says it begins at the cross and ends with resurrection. In the beginning, before the world was made, the God of love planned for redemption that would triumph.

The love of God revealed at Calvary is the love of God revealed at the empty tomb. There is no better place to see love as triumph than in the last chapter of Matthew. The story of the resurrection is told in ten explicit and startling verses. Women come first, just at daybreak, and the empty tomb shakes them to the depth of their being, as Matthew says, "And they departed quickly from the sepulchre with fear and great joy; and did run to bring the disciples word" (Matt. 28:8).

With fear and great joy they did run! There is something arresting about that statement. *With fear and great joy!* Life in microcosm is here—all its hopes and fears, its aspirations and its defeats, its tragedy and its triumph. Life as we know it is a strange mixture of hope and despair, victory and failure, humiliation and triumph, fear and joy, life and death. Sometimes each of us must confront this mixture.

At Calvary, Jesus confronted man's most ancient fears: expediency, compromise, cowardice, opportunism, avarice, betrayal, brutality, death. No man ever faced them so realistically, or confronted them so directly, or challenged them so immediately. The cross was real.

Calvary was neither a joke nor a pageant, and the pain of our life on earth is no academic matter. The enigma of the cross was that the best man the world

had ever known—the kindest, the gentlest, the most
loving, the most courageous—paid with his life for his
love. The passion drives home the truth that man holds
in his hands no incantations to shield himself against
the stark tragedy of life. Life by its very nature makes
us vulnerable, and to care at all is to be exposed. When
we come to the cross, our choices are limited. Like
the thief on Jesus' left, we can end life cursing God
for what life has done to us, or we can end life calling
God "Father" as our Savior did, or like the thief on
the right, we can cast ourselves on the mercy of God.

On that resurrection morning, the first believers ran
with fear, but they also ran with joy. A new redemptive
principle had become real in the world. In the light
of that principle, love's sacrifice made sense. In the
Bible, suffering is never an end of itself; it is always
for a purpose. We do not suffer in vain. Pointless pain
can destroy, but pain for the purpose of healing is not
only endurable but is also cleansing and liberating. A
parent suffers for the welfare of the child, and God's
sacrifice was for the redemption of man. Love is sacrifice and love is redemptive. That is how it triumphs.
Jesus' sacrifice was redemptive, and our love must be
so, lifting up, making better, bringing back to God.

What is the measure of the triumph of the resurrection? Who can verbalize it? For news too good to be
true, perhaps we can best think of running feet and
unbounded joy. The triumph of love manifest in the
resurrection says four wonderful things: light is
stronger than darkness, goodness is stronger than evil,
life is stronger than death, and love is triumphant.

Light is stronger than darkness. Men have always
been afraid of the night; there is so much darkness

around us. Darkness is within and without, submerged, and floating on the surface, paraded and in private, in the heart of the child and the soul of the adult. I recall the story of the five-year-old who loved to go for a drive with his father. Late one afternoon as the shadows were beginning to fall, the little boy's father said, "Bill, go up to your bedroom and get your cap, and we will go for a drive."

Bill was elated until, as he climbed the stairs, it dawned upon him that his bedroom would be engulfed in dusky shadows, and he was afraid of the dark. His steps grew slower and slower. Finally he reached the bedroom door and hesitated. "What's wrong?" called his father. Timidly he admitted his fear of the dark, and his father responded from below, "Well, God is in your bedroom." The listening father heard his five-year-old say through the cracked door, "God, if you are in there, pitch me my cap." Each of us has had such times. We understand fear of dark rooms and fear of the dark places of this world. Darkness may be man's most ancient symbol of evil.

Light has always been a symbol of goodness and truth. The Bible tells us that the believer is a child of light, and his life is lighted by the very light of heaven, a light no darkness can overcome, one which lights every man who comes into the world. Easter's dawn became a symbol for the light of God that is man's only foil for the darkness of the world.

Tell me, how do you empty a room of darkness? You certainly cannot dip it out with a spoon or a shovel. There is only one way—you turn on a light. One is reminded of the child's question, "What is behind the sunset?" And the ready answer, "Tomorrow's dawn."

Resurrection declares that light is stronger than darkness.

Goodness is stronger than evil. The strength of goodness is not always apparent. There are times along our human way when we wonder if evil triumphs. Job was not alone in his quandary, yet each of us knows that, ultimately, evil produces nothing worthwhile and enduring. Only goodness produces that which endures. The apostle Paul declared the most ancient and universal of truths, the heart of the gospel, when he wrote, "Be not overcome of evil, but overcome evil with good" (Rom. 12:21). Goodness overcoming evil is the miracle of the resurrection.

Life is stronger than death. Death we do not understand, but death we know about. It is life's inescapable reality. Every man has a terminal illness or fatal accident. Life is always mortal. No man escapes it alive. Nothing is so inevitable, and to deny it is not realistic.

Death we know about, but death we do not understand. Man has always asked the question, "What is death?" The archaeological ruins of the world reveal that artifacts of funeralia may be the oldest and most universal of all. Why must man die? Man has always wondered. Our questions about death are really questions about life. Does life have meaning? Where does it ultimately lead? If it leads to nothing, then how can it be something? Is death an end to a beginning, or only an ending?

Death wears many faces: stranger, enemy, reliever, friend, door to a larger life. As strange as it may seem, death enhances life. The very limitation it puts on our days makes life more precious. Why are "September Days" so poignant? Because they are so few. Death makes life more precious. You remember the dear one you almost lost? Above all, death confers value on love.

Peter J. Kreeft, in his searching *Love Is Stronger Than Death*, expresses it vividly:

> From youth's point of view, middle age appears as a loss, a diminution to be lamented; but from old age's point of view, it appears as a gift to be appreciated. Remember that a glass filled halfway with water is called half empty if you take for granted its fullness, half full if you do not. Youth takes for granted life and health, and is therefore offended at the half empty cup of days that is middle age and the nearly empty cup that is old age. "Youth is wasted on the young." Youth lives forward, from past to future; its past and present health is the beginning, the assumed point of view, the taken-for-granted standpoint is assessing middle age and aging. Middle age teaches us the great lesson of living backwards, from the future, out of old age and death, appreciating both the life that is gone and the life that is left, noticing the half full cup with eyes that do not take for granted fullness and life and health. Without death there would not be gratitude for life! [1]

No doubt this is what Walter de la Mare meant when he said: "Look thy last on all things lovely every hour." The Christian believer has learned that not only is death our final enemy, but death is the door opening into a fuller life. Indeed our years are filled with it. We must die to be born; to enter a fuller life, we must leave our mother's womb. We must die to infancy to

reach childhood, and youth is only possible when we
reject childhood. The maturity of adulthood is only
possible when we leave our youth. Why should it surprise us that we must die to time to enter eternity?
Resurrection declares that death is but a transition to
a fuller life.

Love is triumph. We began with the admission that
love is sacrifice. It was for God and, sooner or later,
it is for us. This is true of the parent, the husband or
the wife, the friend or the brother, the believer who
ministers in Christ's name in the world.

Love cannot protect itself and be love. However,
such love is ultimately triumph. Why do I say
ultimately? Because otherwise it would simply not be
true. In our present existence, good people don't always get well, achieve economic security, or win. It
is obvious that there are times when evil overcomes
goodness, when the ruthless crush the tender, when
deceit blots out honesty, and when greed dominates
compassion, but our present existence is not the final
chapter. And while life is not always victorious, for
the believer life is always triumphant. Love is invincible because love knows that only God's way heals and
only God's way endures.

Voltaire, that incredible Frenchman with a brilliant
mind, once defined Easter as "a feast celebrated by
Christians in memory of a God who was publicly
hanged." However, the lesson the clever skeptic
missed was that precisely because of His death, life
and immortality have been brought to light through
the gospel. The little girl whose path from school led
by way of a graveyard, when asked if she were afraid,
was nearer the truth in her reply, "No. I just cross it

to reach home." Love that is sacrifice is ultimately love that is triumph.

And so our question is not an ending but a beginning. There must be an exit if there is to be an entrance, and in the mystery and miracle of God's grace, both the entrance and the exit are grounded in love. All creation began in the love of God, and the conquering of the final enemy, death, is done by love's power. In love we were conceived, birthed, and nurtured. Despite our tendency to rebel against the God who made us and reject his divine image stamped within us, he still redeems us and gives us the power of an endless life.

Love is indeed stronger than death because death is merely a temporary detour made necessary by man's sin en route to eternal life. Herein is the centerpiece to the puzzle of man's existence, the ground of his eternal hope!

Notes

Chapter 1.

1. *Broadman Bible Commentary*, Vol. 10, p. 369.
2. *Ibid.*, p. 370.

Chapter 2.

1. Article Nov. 1978, *Commission*, "Toyohiko Kagawa: Going Where Others Do Not," John Allen Moore, p. 19.
2. Charles L. Walks, *A Treasury of Illustration*. Abingdon-Cokesbury, 1950, p. 145.
3. James Hastings, *The Speaker's Bible*, 1 Cor. p. 39, The Speakers Bible Office, Aberdeen, Scotland, 1927.
4. From *The Bible: a New Translation* by James A. R. Moffatt. Copyright © 1935 by Harper and Row Publishers, Inc. Used by permission.
5. James Hastings, *The Speakers Bible*, 1 Cor. p. 47, The Speakers Bible Office, Aberdeen, Scotland, 1927.

Chapter 4.

1. David J. Schwartz, *The Magic of Thinking Big*, New York: Cornerstone Library, p. v.

Chapter 6.

1. Sinclair Lewis, *Elmer Gantry*. A Signet Classic from New American Library, Times Mirror, © 1970, p. 62.
2. In this brief discussion on fields of energy, I am indebted to an article, "Creativity" by James Vargin, p. 21 ff., published in *Synthesis 3–4, The Realization of the Self,* The Synthesis Press, 830 Woodside Road, Redwood City, Calif. 94061.
3. Karl A. Menninger, *Love Against Hate*. New York: Harcourt, Brace & Jovanovich, 1959.
4. Karl A. Menninger, *Menninger Perspective,* Winter & Spring 1979, The Menninger Foundation, Box 829, Topeka, Kansas 66601.

Chapter 7.

1. This author has made every effort to find this source of this quotation.

Chapter 8.

1. Corrie ten Boom and Carole C. Carlson, *In My Father's House*. Old Tappan, N.J.: Fleming H. Revell, © 1976, p. 15. Used by permission.
2. Corrie ten Boom, *Prison Letters*. Old Tappan, N.J.: Fleming H. Revell, © 1975, p. 17.
3. *Ibid.*, p. 18.
4. *Ibid.*, p. 19.
5. *Ibid.*, p. 26.
6. *Ibid.*, p. 80.
7. *Ibid.*, p. 81.
8. Phil. 2:5.

Chapter 9.

1. Corrie ten Boom with John and Elizabeth Sherrill, *The Hiding Place*. Lincoln, Va.: Chosen Books. Copyright © 1971, p. 47.
2. *Ibid*.

Chapter 10.

1. Elizabeth O'Connor, *The New Community*, Harper and Row, © 1976, p. 3.

Chapter 12.

1. Peter J. Kreeft, New York: Harper and Row, *Love Is Stronger Than Death*, pps. 49–50. Used by permission.